# PONDERINGS

*A journey of healing*

*through intimacy with Jesus*

## MICHELE M. STYLC

Ponderings

Scripture taken from the HOLY BIBLE, NEW INTERNATIONAL VERSION ®. Copyright© 1973, 1978, 1984 by International Bible Society. Used by permission of Zondervan Publishing House. All rights reserved.

The "NIV" and "New International Version" trademarks are registered in the United States. Patent and Trademark Office by International Bible Society. Use of either trademark requires the permission of International Bible Society.

Adoration image in Closing Thoughts used with express permission from David Bowman- Artist.

This novel is a work of nonfiction.

Published by Praise and Glory Press.

Cover and interior design by Raney Day Creative, LLC.

ISBN# 978-0-578-84640-8

Printed in the United States of America.

*God made two great lights- the greater light to govern the day, and the lesser light to govern the night. He also made the stars.*

*Genesis 1:16*

*Those who are wise will shine like the brightness of the heavens, and those who lead many to righteousness like the stars forever and ever.*

*Daniel 12 :3*

*Lift up your eyes and look to the heavens: who created all these? He who brings out the starry hosts one by one and calls forth each of them by name. Because of His great power and mighty strength, not one of them is missing.*

*Isaiah 40:26 (Life in the Spirit Study Bible)*

*Reader's Note: The Biblical references within this book come from the New International Version unless otherwise stated.*

# TABLE OF CONTENTS

# INTRODUCTION

Throughout my life, I have spent countless amounts of time pondering about what the future holds, what the past has meant, and where my path will take me. While I have learned, maybe a little late, to instead hold conversations with the Lord and the Holy Spirit about these things, I know they are showing me the answers and are literally connecting the dots of my life experiences to find the meaning I've always been searching for. Many times, when these moments occur, I find myself having a palpable "Aha" response.

This book was birthed as a result of those, "Aha" moment experiences. God clearly directed me to record and share them rather than waste their pain or meaning. For some, my Aha moments will just confirm how gracious our God is to those who continually seek Him. (Jeremiah 29:13) For others, who may complain about not getting answers or hearing from the Lord, I can assure them that He has not changed His address or phone number. Early in my journey, I distinctly remember asking the Lord why I was able to hear His Spirit when it seemed so difficult for others. His reply was, "You look for Me."

In writing these Aha moments, the reader will discover what I asked and what He revealed to me. Some are revelations uncovered during quiet times with Him. They've occurred at night when I can't sleep or when watching the stars. (I love the clear star-studded skies!) Sometimes God's revelations came during housework, driving, or other daily activities. This book is not designed to spark debate over beliefs or philosophy. I pray for you, my readers, that as you read what I have shared through my life's journey, you will understand that these experiences are not coincidences, fabrications, or of little importance. There are NO coincidences with God!

I realized that storytelling was a God given destiny when I became a teacher. Stories were one of my students' favorite things. The changes in my voice and my larger-than-life gestures had them on the edge of their seats. They waited for my stories daily. God doesn't waste a drop of what is deposited within us. That storytelling skill was practiced and polished throughout more than thirty-eight years of teaching, for an audience that begged for more. It gave me the confidence I so desperately needed for this next leg of the journey that He called me to walk.

I hope you will discover your own truths through your relationship with Jesus; that as you ponder your own experiences, He is faithful and gracious to give you your own Aha moments. Take His hand and begin your journey with anticipation and confidence!

# A PRAYER FOR YOU, THE READER

*Father God, I am living proof of the amazing love and healing You hold for Your precious children. I lift each reader of this book before Your throne and ask that You will work on their behalf to put every piece in place for their healing to occur. Raise them up to walk through the valleys and atop the turbulent waters of their lives. Give them the strength and courage they need to face the issues that are holding them back from all You have destined for them to become. Show them the way You see things and let them feel the strength that comes from placing their troubles in Your hands. Create in them renewal and wholeness. Teach them to trust You for their todays and tomorrows. Go before them, beside them, and be their rear guard. Protect them on their journey and provide what is needed so they receive total healing, through every part of the trip. Finally, bless them with the saving grace and knowledge of who You are, so they may spend eternity with You in the heavenly courts above. Thank you for each of them. I pray these things in the name of Your Son, Jesus. AMEN!*

# ACKNOWLEDGEMENTS

I would like to extend my sincere gratitude to the following blessed souls who have supported me as I publish my first book:

**Chandra** - You came alongside without hesitation to lend your wisdom and expertise to me, a new writer. It means more to me than you can imagine. It reminded me of the times I opened my classroom door to so many students who were led to become educators. I felt it was my responsibility to give them a hand up just as you extended your hand to me. May you be richly rewarded by the Lord for helping me to share His goodness with others.

**Kendall** - You were brave enough to read the very first drafts of each story and gave me the courage to keep writing. I loved watching your facial expressions as you read about God's goodness to me. You are so dear to my heart and His! I am confident He will pour countless blessings into your life because of your selflessness for others. I will be waiting to write about those experiences!

**Susan** - What a blessing you are in my life right now! God placed you in my path for so many amazing reasons. Thank you for being such a wonderful listener and encourager. I looked forward to sharing stories with you each week and was lifted up by your laughter and comments. Thank you for making the connection between Chandra and myself. I didn't know how all of the pieces would be put in place, but He knew exactly who to ask to orchestrate them. You are a dear sister in the Lord.

**David Bowman** - What an honor you granted me to have one of your breathtaking pictures within my first book! As I finished the Closing Thoughts story, I searched for an image of Jesus that would capture the feelings within my heart at that moment. When I saw your picture entitled Adoration, it took my breath away. Thank you for taking the time to speak with me and for allowing me to use your soul stirring work!

David's work can be found at www.davidbowmanart. com. Please visit this amazing site and discover his awe-inspiring artwork!

**Becky and Shelli** - Thank you for your willingness to 'test drive' the book and provide honest feedback to enhance it for others. There were certain elements I was striving to share and your comments allowed me to measure how each was addressed and handled. It is my heart's desire to touch the hearts of others so they take hold of healing opportunities in their lives. The personal remarks you shared about your own journeys with Jesus and the stories in the book, have strengthened my confidence in accomplishing this goal. May you each be blessed as you continue on your pondering journeys with Jesus!

**Astrid** - I will be forever grateful for the time and energy you gave to this book editing each story with the heart of God. You not only looked for things that needed correction, you considered those who would be reading these stories and suggested changes that would bring souls to Jesus! I know that He is pleased with all that you gave to this assignment. Without a doubt, I am sure that His words to you would be, "Well done, good and faithful servant!" Thank you for sharing in this journey and being a dear friend!

**Tom** - My precious knight! You have encouraged and believed in me for many, many years. No matter where our journey has taken us, you have staunchly been at my side. You have always done everything in your power to provide whatever I needed for my career, ministry work, things dear to my heart, and our family. My greatest ally, encouraging me to push on, even when I was my own worst enemy. As I wrote the stories in this book, I became even more grateful God gave me such a wonderful soul mate. Thank you for teaching me to not settle for what life hands us, but to seek what it is God desires for us to have from our experiences. Because of you, I am sure my box in heaven will have little left in it or nothing at all! I love you my treasured knight!

# DEDICATION

*THIS BOOK IS DEDICATED TO*

**Jesus** - Thank you for the desire that continually grows within me to know more and more about You. Thank you for giving me the path to write for You, compose songs for You, and become a minister of Your Word. I pray all I do brings You glory and honor and brings souls into the saving knowledge and grace of who You are. I am privileged to serve You and be known as Yours!

**My husband, Tom** - You've believed in me and remained faithful to our life together through good times and bad. You are my knight in shining armor and my protector. I thank God for your heart, integrity, and passion to live your life for the Lord. You fill my days with true love. I am honored to be your wife, your LADY, and best friend. My heart is yours forever!

*June 14, 1981- When the Knight and his Princess rode off into the glorious sunset of a lifetime of love together!*

**Deb** - You were a shining light on a hill when I needed direction the most. I will always love you as a sister, a confidant, a mother, and a friend. You taught me to see God in my life and believe I am truly a valued daughter of the King whom He genuinely loves. I desire to be obedient to Him as I write this book and know you're smiling in

heaven as I finally get to work. Thank you for pushing me to be all that He has called me to be.

Deb, you were indeed a blessing!

# IN THE BEGINNING

Every journey has a beginning. As you begin, I thought it might be helpful to give you a snapshot of where I was as a high school senior at John Carroll. A lot of the hurts in my life were coming 'to a full boil' during this time. Many pieces of my life were fragile and insecure. My self-concept was in tatters. I was suffering from the silent abandonment of a first love that I never saw coming. It was the first time I had given a piece of my heart to someone and allowed myself to be vulnerable. The results devastated me.

It was also during this time I wrote a lot. I found tranquility in writing and it was a good distraction from my anxieties.

Every worthwhile effort has a starting point; a place to look back and reflect on how far we've come. Below is a poem that I wrote as a senior in 1975. It was published in our student literary magazine, The Pinnacle. The Lord had me retrieve it because it so vividly gave a picture of how much I was hurting. I think this poem will also allow you to have a deeper appreciation of all that He does to rescue the one lamb who is missing, when He has the other 99. (Luke 15:4-6) Without the Lord, I emphatically know that I would never have been able to celebrate who I am today. Thank you, Lord Jesus!

*Good Morning Darkness,*
*All the sunshine gone away.*
*All my laughter has now ended,*
*I've got nothing more to say.*

*Good Morning Darkness,*
*What will we do today?*
*Build castles on the seashore,*
*And have them washed away?*

*Good Morning Darkness,*
*Are you still behind my mind?*
*Will you listen to me ever?*
*Shall I leave my heart behind?*

*Good Morning Darkness,*
*Have you found a friend for me?*
*Have you looked among the mountains?*
*Through the forests, by the sea?*

*Good Morning Darkness,*
*Don't bother, drop my plea.*
*I didn't mean to trouble you,*
*It means nothing now to me.*

*Spring, 1975*

# COVENANT

Covenant is of extreme importance to God. Our covenant relationship with Him was so vital, that after years of dealing with the Israelites, He realized His chosen people could not keep His laws or attain what He desired. Because of His unfailing love, He made a way where there seemed to be no way. (Isaiah 43:16-19) He sent His only Son, as the sacrifice for each of us, so the covenant relationship He longed for and desired, was accomplished despite our weaknesses and shortcomings. (John 3:16)

*

**An Essential Dot:** I remember so clearly getting ready to take our beloved dog Cheyenne down to the veterinarian, one Saturday morning. A question crossed my mind about a couple that my husband Tom and I knew, who had recently gone through a bitter divorce. I asked the Lord, "What went wrong there?" He distinctly said, "There was no covenant." "Hmmm," I thought and hurried to get going. However, God had other plans.

God continued to impress the word "covenant" upon my mind. Then He added, "Tell your Pastor what I have said." I agreed but explained to God that if I stopped now, I would be late for my fifty-five-minute trip to the veterinarian. "I'll do it when I get back," I thought. God would have none of it. So, I quickly got on the computer and emailed our Pastor. When I arrived at the veterinarian's office, an ear-to-ear smile was triggered when I realized that I was five minutes early for the appointment. After a great visit there, we headed home.

✳

The word "covenant" would become a cornerstone in my faith journey and relationship with the Lord. I had no idea of its importance then, and continue to learn about its significance. Covenant is the essence of your relationship with God. It is the beginning and the eternal of the perfect intimacy of communion with Him. Realizing its establishment and importance is no less significant than building on solid rock instead of sinking sand. (Matthew 7:24-27) The Lord had given me a foundational truth that morning that would anchor my life to Him for eternity.

A question to consider: What kind of love is it that the Son of Man would lay down His own life for me?

# LOOKING FOR GOD EVERYDAY
## The Passionate Pursuit

The Bible says that God is omnipresent which means that He is everywhere all the time. Do you look for God? You should daily. He is waiting to be found by each one of us. I often tell Him aloud, "I see Your fingerprints!"

I believe God genuinely enjoys our seeking Him. He delights in our longing for more of all He is and will be to us. I have felt His smile and know He has a sense of humor. There are times Jesus and I are working on an issue and when I am close to understanding another piece, I can imagine Him leaning forward on the throne and saying to His Father, "Look- look! She's going to get it!"

During my journey to heal from hurts of the past, turning to God became even more meaningful to me. As I worked with Deb, a friend and counselor, she would say to me, "Michele, it's so important that you get this!" I continue to learn more even though some things will not be understood until I am safely home. God longs for my pursuit, and He lavishly blesses me because of it.

Sometimes people try too hard to hear or feel God.

He does not make it hard for us to find Him. His only requirement is we seek Him with our whole heart. He promises when we do, we will find Him. (Jeremiah 29:13)

*

**Another dot:** I met my husband Tom in July of 1976. I was not looking for anyone at the time. I was still nursing a very broken heart with *no* intentions of allowing myself to be vulnerable again. It was my girlfriend who wanted me to see the new beau she was crazy about.

Things became awkward when we rode by his house on a dead-end street and he was outside working on his truck. Of course, she had to stop!

The problem became worse when he showed more interest in me and getting my phone number, than her lovestruck conversation.

After about 30 minutes, I convinced him he had the right number (which he did not), and we were on our way.

However, having the wrong phone number did not stop Tom. About a week later, he appeared at my front door, smiling from ear-to-ear!

I politely told him I was not interested, shared I did not want to hurt my friend, and thanked him for stopping by. I believed I would never see him again. I was wrong.

Next, began Tom's daily drives up and down my road, several times each morning and evening. He traveled my road faithfully.

After about two weeks, my Mom convinced me to go on one date with him. She hoped it would be enough to end the daily road trips.

Two weeks later, after a few dates, he presented me with an engagement ring! I was in shock. While I did not accept it then, I did much later with the regret that I had made him wait so long.

He knew he had found the love of his life, and nothing was going to deter him from securing the covenant for a lifetime! I was, and still am, blessed he was willing to wait for me.

*

That passionate pursuit and fervor is exactly how we should go after God because He is the lover of our souls. He will also wait, no matter how long it takes, for us to acknowledge Him as Lord and Savior, because it is all that matters to Him – a covenant for an eternal lifetime. (Exodus 34:14, 2Chronicles16:9, Isaiah 40:11, Zephaniah 3:17)

What are you waiting for?

Tell God that you are on the lookout for Him; His footprints, fingerprints, even the warmth of His embrace Then, be still and wait. He will NOT disappoint. (Psalm 46:10)

# EXTRAVAGANT LOVE

## 1 JOHN 3:1

My husband Tom is an extravagant giver. I have watched him, throughout the years, work himself to the bone to support our family and bless me with the things he knows I cherish.

I often tell friends I had to stop admiring things when we were dating or out shopping, because I would be the proud owner of those objects within twenty-four hours. More than once, he tossed stones at my bedroom window screen to get my attention, and send new goodies up with a rope.

Tom's devotion to being a blessing doesn't stop with blessing me. He listens intently to our friends as they share ideas or needs with their own projects. Many of them know if they mention something they're looking for, Tom will make it a priority to help them find it.

One of my fondest memories was right after we moved into our brand-new home in 1983. I always wanted a silver-gray Pontiac Firebird. That car sent chills up my spine. I longed to cruise around in it with my long hair blowing in the breeze.

One Saturday, as I was completing my house cleaning routines, a car horn beeped in front of our house. As I peeked out from a window, there was my Tom smiling from ear-to-ear in a gorgeous gray Firebird. He waved me out and I went shaking my head in disbelief. "Take it back!" was all I could say over and over. "I will, after you test drive it," was his response. I'd like to say that it took a lot of convincing for me to take it for a spin, but it didn't.

As I settled into the driver's seat, Tom stood on the curb with complete satisfaction all over his face. This would certainly qualify for at least one hundred points on the scoreboard with Michele!

Hesitantly, I took it the short distance up the street and turned around. He was waiting for me as I came back down. "That's the best you got?" he challenged. So, I decided to ramp up my game and took off down the street to a nearby cul-de-sac of homes. I was laughing and shaking at the same time.

By the time I turned back onto the main street of the development, there were two men standing in the street waiting for me. Waving their arms and shaking their heads they screamed, "We have kids in this neighborhood, what's wrong with you?" I waved and meekly drove back to our house. Don't miss the irony here- they could see where we lived (I was their neighbor) and I was a teacher- a caretaker of children.

Tom's giving and intent are selfless. There is immense joy when he gives delight to others. His fulfillment comes from fulfilling someone else. While he has loved his trucks and equipment all his life, they have been the means to an end, to support his family and give to others.

It is no wonder that when I once asked God about loving Tom, He simply replied, "Love the heart of the man!" That puts him in a rather high-ranking with other people in scripture whose hearts God loved.

*

God is the extravagant giver of all time! There are sure to be many thoughts and opinions about that remark. Some will be so burdened by the wrongs of their lives, that they will adamantly deny this is true. I understand and can appreciate their pain and limited perspective. However, it is through my pain and healing I discovered the countless gifts that God has poured into my life.

When we went through the marriage classes, before our wedding, we learned about 'wants' and 'needs.' We thought it was childish for adults to seriously consider these things. However, it didn't take long before the list of wants didn't quite fit into the budget of the needs.

God is an expert at our wants and needs. Each one of us has debated with Him over what we want, not only the material things, but their timing as well. We often expect Him to meet our needs, without asking or thanking Him for them. What we forget, is that expressing our wants is not the core of what God is yearning for when we spend time together.

His word expressly says that He is very aware of what we need. Remembering the difference between wants and needs, helps mature believers to realize God is more concerned with meeting our needs.

That is what should be more important to us, as well. He often told His disciples to travel with the barest of supplies. They learned to depend on Him for everything. (Philippians 4:11-13)

✳

During one of our recent conversations, I shared with Tom that some of my deepest moments with him, have occurred when we just cuddle close together and talk. There is nothing as comforting to me as the warmth of his arms around me. We can talk to each other about anything, and have learned how to help one another over the rough spots in our journeys. We've asked for forgiveness from one another and learned to protect each other from moments that might cause pain or sorrow. Tom has carried my cross (my burdens) for me when I couldn't, as I have for him.

While all the gifts Tom has blessed me with, hold warm places in my heart, the most precious gifts have been those that I needed - just like my Father in heaven! As a Michele expert, He knows how to gently open my heart and deposit in exact measure just what is needed. When He does, I am content- wants are never considered.

At one point in our journey, Tom and I discovered one night while praying, that thanking God for blessings fell short of what He was providing. We now thank Him for blessings seen and unseen. Just think about how many things His hand has saved you from. Pretty scary to consider, don't you think?

When we lived in Crossroads, PA, I used to sit in my favorite swing and spend quiet time with Jesus. During one of those times, I found myself contemplating the enormity of all He had done in my life to bless and protect me. The realization of this provision inspired me to create a song in which I asked what I could do to bless Him. It was composed within the moments it took for me to sing it. Without hesitation, the next verses came streaming through my lips. In return, He asked what He could do for me as my Father to bless me. Below is a short piece of that song. What a powerful exchange between Father and daughter!

*What can I do for You my Father?*
*How can I bless You today?*
*I'll walk the path laid before me,*
*Follow each step of Your way.*

*For it is my heart's desire,*
*To do what You ask,*
*Your perfect will.*
*I'll sit and wait for You, Jesus,*
*I'll keep my heart very still.*

*What can I do for you my daughter?*
*How can I bless you today?*
*I'll lay the path out before you,*
*Guide you each step of the way.*

*For it is My heart's desire,*
*To give what you ask,*

*In My perfect will.*
*I'll sit and wait for you daughter,*
*I'll keep my heart very still.*

# FAITH IN GOD

Why is faith in God so difficult?
We easily believe in other things in our lives and stand quite firm on them. Truth, love, beauty, justice, loyalty, the list goes on. Many of these things cannot be seen or touched, yet these are the same attributes that we say make it hard for us to put our faith in God.

What is the difference?

Is it just convenient to make that claim, shifting the blame, or excusing ourselves from what we cannot see, touch, understand or explain? Maybe our lack of faith is just because we don't always get our way, or the results aren't what we planned on or expected.

The same is true for what we daily choose to believe. Most of us have a certain TV news station we listen to because of the believability of the news presented by its anchor men and women. Why is it easier for us to believe a human being conveying information they received from another human being (probably more than one), but not the truth in the infallible word of God?

God has touched my life and answered countless prayers - many more than I could ever share. Does He always do it in my timing or my desired result? No. Is it easy, comfortable, or secure? Most times, it's challenging, concerning, and sometimes I'm shaking inside and out. But He is always faithful! Even in my most desperate moments, I have had to stand on His faithfulness. God just is faithful and it cannot be denied. Will I struggle again? Of course, I'm flesh. But He is God and I couldn't be in better hands!

More than once, I've listened to women whom I admire because of their relationship with God, tell others to keep a journal. This journal should record prayers said, answers received, visions, dreams, etc., as altars in memorial of your relationship with Jesus. (Explore why the Israelites built altars to the Lord in the desert to understand this significance.)

While this act of journaling should be essential for every believer, I think it serves a single, greater purpose. It becomes the believer's Faith Testament. Within its pages, are the undeniable records of the covenant journey between the Savior and the saved.

Without dispute, they lay the solid rocks of the foundation of faith needed to move mountains in the life of a believer. They take them toward a deeper understanding and unshakeable confidence that He can indeed do the impossible. (Matthew 19:23-30)

My journal has the title, "Faithfulness Journal." On the inside cover, are the words of the wonderful hymn, "Great is Thy Faithfulness." I keep it in my night stand and it's there whenever I need a reminder that He has indeed been faithful and supplied all I have needed, even when I don't see it His way.

Several years ago, my husband Tom and I were invited by dear friends to view a documentary, by Evangelist Reinhard Bonnke, that gave first person accounts of believers who had physically died but were brought back to life. Those believers shared their experiences about heaven and what they saw and heard. One man in particular was highlighted as he shared that the Lord had allowed him to return to share an important revelation. His story was based on one profound point. There were groups of people he saw who were not given entry into heaven and when he questioned why, he was told, "They did not believe." He was then instructed to come back to earth and share this message so that many who were nonbelievers would be saved and enter heaven for eternity.

Romans 8:34 and 10:9-13 clearly explains the necessary requirement for an eternity in heaven: Belief in Jesus Christ as the Son of God; and belief in His death, resurrection, and placement at the right hand of the Father. It is important to note a life of works (just doing good things) does little if anything to gain our way into heaven. That does not mean God does not want us to live a life for Him - this is an expectation; it is why we are here. However, works are not at the root of our covenant. Your belief in Him is the key!

# FROM THE MOUTHS
# OF BABES

Have you ever wondered why Jesus reprimanded the disciples for prohibiting the little children to come to Him? After having the privilege of teaching over eight hundred children in my career, I am quite sure it was because He didn't have to deal with all the baggage, we older children have accumulated!

Children inherently trust and want to please those who look over them. They haven't been muddied by everything that vies for our attention. They are pure and open to learning about life and the world around them. They're not afraid to ask the challenging questions and expect us to know all the answers. They are perfectly content with a surprise snack during the day, extra minutes at play time, and of course, no homework. I sometimes surprised my students by eating lunch with them in the cafeteria. You would have thought I gave them a million dollars!

At times, there were tough things to deal with, but most of the time our classroom was a safe community. We often talked about the gifts the students possessed and how they could use them later in life. As we developed into a classroom family, they saw how each of their gifts became valuable to the whole family. I wanted them to believe in themselves at an early age and not struggle as I had for so much of my life.

I took my responsibility as a teacher very seriously. At the Back-to-School night events or during parent conferences, I told parents that I was literally signing my name on the life of each student. It was my responsibility to make sure they received every opportunity to achieve their best during their year with me. I genuinely loved my job and looked forward to each new day with my students. They were precious and priceless.

That all sounds awesome, doesn't it? Believe it or not, I almost allowed all of those wonderful events and memories to never happen. However, the children He put in my path had different ideas.

*

During my first years of college, I was offered a position as an instructional assistant. It began as a part-time position which worked well with my college schedule. Unfortunately, it was also about this same time that events at home became increasingly difficult with responsibilities that had to be addressed.

I made the decision to place the needs of my family before what was important to my future. I was determined to do what needed to be done to try to keep my parents and brothers happy and have life be somewhat normal and meaningful. I share this only because it was what I wanted to do, not to take any credit or invite gratitude.

There were many times that college took a back seat or even found itself in the trunk of my car because of this choice. Even though I found my calling of teaching while working part-time at the elementary school, my heart's cry was to make the difference in my family. My efforts to make everything work at home grew at the same rate as my frustrations of never succeeding. As a result, my college aspirations became an added casualty. Suffice it to say, there was a huge price to pay for that decision.

During the time I attended classes, there were two professors who boldly declared that they thought I had what it took to become a teacher, but they didn't believe I would make it. The assignments and projects I submitted showed creativity and potential. I was keenly aware of the capabilities of different levels of students and techniques to address special needs learners. I remember sitting on the floor of my boyfriend Tom's bedroom one Sunday afternoon working on a measuring lesson for a group of third graders. We measured and cut hundreds of neon straw lengths for the students. They used them to follow directions to create their own Halloween skeleton. It was time consuming, but well worth the effort as I watched students engrossed in the measuring activities. While I was able to give this project my all, there were other times when class assignments only received minimal attention. Getting siblings to school, dealing with laundry or cleaning, or working to resolve the latest items of contention at home were more pressing priorities. The comments of these professors only evaluated what was evident on the surface and temporarily pushed me further away from my God appointed destiny.

In 1980, Tom asked me to spend the rest of my life with him. He waited for four years as I tried to rescue something that wasn't my responsibility. He wanted to start our life together many times before, but gave me the time I needed to dedicate my life totally to him.

Once again, God began to align the pieces of His design for my life. My position with the school system, as an instructional assistant, became full-time and I had resigned myself to the fact that I would remain there until a ripe old age. An exceptional group of students however, had a much different plan.

There were two classes of students I taught at that time. I worked with the primary students in the morning and the intermediate group in the afternoon. We focused each day on the three Rs (Reading, wRiting, and aRithmetic), and finding the tools that enabled each student to learn them with success. The teacher who had the older group had become ill and had to take an extended leave of absence. I had the responsibility of writing and organizing each day's set of substitute plans for that class. One day, the principal called me into his office and offered me the long-term position for this class, sharing that I was capable of handling the responsibilities. After all, I was already doing most of what was needed. I was honored, but declined. When the students found out I didn't take the position, they were furious!

Bluntly, they asked me why. I shared I didn't think I had what it took to teach them every day. Now you should also know I had spent day after day telling them to go after what they wanted in life and never allow anyone to dictate what they would accomplish. It only took seconds for them to serve me a huge helping of my own words. They were not ready to just accept the circumstances as they were. Their next questions required my sharing with them how I would go back to college and finish my degree. Holiday break was approaching quickly, so I told them I would visit the college over the break.

I believed they would forget when school resumed. No such luck. I was in even deeper water when I shared, I had not gone to the college. So began a period of the children not speaking to me. It wasn't long before I found myself attending classes and working to finish my degree. And, to my delight, my experiences within the classrooms, qualified me to earn student teaching credits without further classwork.

*

Those students believed in me and wouldn't let me 'off the hook' until I had returned to complete my dream. Their pure trust in me gave me a clear picture of why Jesus encouraged those children to gather around Him – the children knew that with Him all things are possible. It is never too late on His clock.

Looking back, the girl who put her own desires on hold and then almost forgot them, became the woman who graduated with honors and added credits in a minor area. I went on to be a light on a hill to hundreds of students who were put in my care. There were nominations and awards presented for the work I had done. However, my greatest joy was to share in the moments as I sat among my students, listening and teaching them to be all they were designed to be - just as Jesus had so long ago.

Right before I completed my degree, Whitney Houston's song, *One Moment in Time* became popular. The chorus of that song was very special to me.

The words were the realization of what I had accomplished. I had become more than I thought I could be, but it was no surprise to my students. It's a good thing they didn't have the ability to communicate with the two professors who believed I wouldn't accomplish my dream. They saw the gifts God had placed inside their teacher and were not afraid to expect me to put those gifts to use.

My students were not the only ones smiling over me. When I crossed the stage on commencement day in 1995, there were two rousing voices from the audience that celebrated my accomplishment - my knight Tom and my therapist Dr. E. While my father was in attendance that day and my heart yearned for his approval, he made the choice to remain silent. There were no words shared between us.

The license plate on my car is a constant reminder of that one moment in time. It says:

**1MMTNTM**: 1 (one), MMT (moment), N (in), TM (time). It is also quite a conversation starter as countless numbers of people stop and try to figure out what it means!

Thank you, Jesus, that you always welcome Your children to sit at Your feet and learn from the Master!

# THE POWER OF WORDS

Weight has been an issue for me all my life. I sometimes look at the pictures I have from when I was younger and wonder what happened. Some people will tell you that if you can name a problem, you're on your way to solving it. While naming is an essential part of the puzzle, I don't agree it's always the key to resolution.

I knew I had a problem with staying at a healthy weight. My father brutally reminded me of it, often. I knew girls around me didn't have a weight issue, but I didn't know why I did. It has been a hurdle for me as long as I can remember.

At my Dad's viewing, I was shocked to hear my fourth-grade teacher share that she never saw me as 'heavy.' I had a larger frame and she thought I carried it well. It still makes me smile to remember my grandfather saying that he liked women who had something to hold on to! But, oh, there were so many others who let me know I wasn't desirable.

My wedding day was the most important day of my life. It was the beginning of my life with my Tom. He had waited patiently for me for four and a half long years while I tried to fix my family without avail. I was more important to him than his own life. And, it was the chance I had waited for all my life. Now I could prove to myself I could have a warm, loving, presentable home. So many anticipated firsts, right at my fingertips. I even asked him if we could stay on our honeymoon and not return home. It was a dream come true.

Life was amazing during those first years! I quickly became the happiest wife around as my knight arrived home each night and we planned for the future.

Two years after we were married, we bought our first brand new home. White picket fences were sure to be the next project. I was beginning to believe I was going to make a terrific teacher and couldn't wait to have our own little cherubs.

Yet again, those words from the past came at me. After sharing our desire, my OB/GYN had sternly announced to me that no weight loss would result in serious medical issues. She had no right to declare those things over my life. However, that was the kind of language I was accustomed to. Believing what she spoke over me as truth, I began a year-long journey of daily walks through all kinds of weather.

At my next annual visit, I was elated to share my sixty-five-pound weight loss! Her nurses and staff were so thrilled and beside themselves with congratulations. My heart was pounding as the doctor came into the exam room. She noted the loss and without expression, told me more was necessary. I left deflated and empty. Surely God would bless us with our own children when He had given me such teaching gifts for the children of others.

A few years later, we discovered with immense joy, we were expecting our first child! It was a glorious surprise! But not for everyone. Once again, the doctor cautioned me with a pointed finger to not get excited about the pregnancy. This time, I was determined she wasn't going to steal my joy. I left with expectation and a smile.

In less than a week, we were back in her office to hear the devastating news that we had a new angel in heaven. Words cannot explain what we felt at that moment. Indescribable pain. Where were my white picket fences? Hadn't I worked hard enough growing up? Where had I failed? There were other incomprehensible events that occurred that day. The doctor decided to begin the necessary operation without waiting for an anesthesiologist and I woke up during the procedure. I was placed in a recovery room next to a woman, who was also named Michele, who had just had her baby. The first thing I heard was her nurse saying, "Michele, wake up. You've had a beautiful baby boy!" These are just a few of the incomprehensible events. Tom and I held onto one another with only unanswered questions and wounded hearts.

While I have only shared a snapshot of our treatment that day, I do know that God was with us every moment. I must also mention that the medical issues the doctor was sure were going to send me to the graveyard, never occurred.

In subsequent visits to this doctor's office, I found myself in a familiar place. Surrounded by women who were still expecting children, an outsider with no understanding of why or how to get it right the next time. Having failed, with no explanation why, I felt withdrawn from the others, put off to the side and alone.

After the miscarriage, to put it politely, I fell off a cliff. Tom came home one day to find me in a fetal ball, in the corner of our kitchen. He tenderly wrapped me in his arms and we began the long, painful journey back to living life with meaning.

I worked with an amazing psychologist for seven years. He helped me understand many pieces of the shattered mess that had long before been in the corner of that kitchen. Somewhere during those many hours of talking, listening, searching, and understanding, he gave me a homework assignment: "Watch the movie, *Pretty Woman*," he said. "When you come in the next time, we'll talk about it."

I have owned that movie, ever since it was a homework assignment. The entire story was meaningful to me, but he was interested in my hearing and learning from one specific scene - when Julia Roberts shares her growing up memories with Richard Gere while in a tub filled with bubble bath. Roberts responds to Gere's questions about what she had been told during that time about herself. Her reply was, "When you've been told something all of your life, you begin to believe it is true."

The power of words. The Bible is correct when it shares that the power of death and life is held within the tongue. (Proverbs 18:21) The spoken word, so easily doled out, yet how many ever measure or temper it for impact?

I later understood I had buried myself deep within my own body, to shield myself from the pain around me. While I had an amazing protector and partner at my side, I still believed what those self-righteous people had said about me was true. Before Tom, I didn't feel loved, nor did I think I deserved to be loved. When I worked up the courage to reach out for love, others judged my efforts as minimal or silently walked away.

I withdrew further and further inside of myself. My growing up years weren't a time of excitement and memories. Many times, they were agony. I never felt able to join in or anticipate social activities with the freedom others my age seemed to exercise so easily. They never seemed burdened with family issues that carried more importance or had to be maneuvered around. I remember traveling to high school for my senior retreat weekend terrified that I would miss the bus. My father was at the wheel as my mother and I endured his bitter remarks for the hour-long trip. Matters were made more tense because we were late, as usual. While I made the bus, by the time we had arrived at the retreat center, my nerves were so undone that I spent most of the weekend in the bathroom unable to keep anything down. Little by little, I was swallowed by the dysfunction surrounding me.

Tom was an outstretched arm in a typhoon. He held onto me for dear life. He endured the times I didn't trust to take his hand, because of the past abandonment. He came at the lies I believed with deliberate resolve, to prove to me they were wrong.

✳

I taught in a public-school system thirty-eight and a half years. I made a promise to God that if He opened the door for me in those buildings, I would walk through them and shine His light. He gave me many opportunities. I was blessed to see His hand at work in the lives of the children I taught, even though I was still working on getting rid of the baggage from my past.

I thought I was pretty clever at making the most important rule of my room, to treat other people the way you want to be treated. To seal the deal, I copied the rule on yellow paper and had the kiddies glue it into one of their notebooks on the first day of school. Each year, we followed the same routine, until one year when one of my new cherubs raised his hand and said, "Mrs. Stylc, I know why you put it on yellow paper. It's the Golden Rule!" I smiled with joy as the other kids acknowledged the discovery.

We had an understanding- we all knew where it came from - and it was the line that meant trouble if you crossed it with another person. The children also learned that it included the words they spoke to one another.

I am proud to say my students became keenly aware of the power their words had over one another. They were also devastated when they crossed the line and had disappointed me. They learned how to measure their responses to situations and consider the feelings of others in what was said or heard. The phrase, 'if you can't say anything nice, don't say anything at all,' was heard often in our classroom.

Words are powerful - God created the entire world with His spoken word. Speak with wisdom because what you say or refrain from saying, may shape the existence of another human being and give them either a lifetime of pain or joy.

# WHAT'S IN A NAME?

Even before we take our first breath outside the womb, a lifetime identifier has been bestowed upon us - a name. How that name is chosen depends upon tradition, legacy, emotions, or a multitude of other factors.

While those on earth are most times beside themselves with pride and joy at the arrival of a new life, the Lord Himself delights in the new creation, fashioned in His own image, much more. He calls us, "His beloved", "cherished", "chosen", to name a few!

Once we have arrived and embarked upon our journey, certain dreams and expectations also come with the territory. In my growing years, I allotted countless hours, days and years to making my name meaningful to others including colleagues, administrators, professors, and family.

As a society, we usually determine a person's worth on the number of letters that are stacked at the end of their name. While to some degree continued education is necessary, the reality of why we pursue it, is sometimes lost within the swollen heads and puffed egos of those who obtain it.

It may be outside of your grasp to believe that the Lord has a chosen name for each of His children. He does! His pride over each of us is also well outside of our carnal understanding. He places us on the earth with a divine purpose to fulfill and just like many earthly parents, gives us the free will to pursue our own paths. His desire is, through a masterfully designed relationship with Him, that we seek His divine purpose for our lives. When that goal is revealed, the true design for our creation unfolds. It took many years for me to discover the many precious names God had whispered to me. This realization was the result of the establishment and nurturing of a relationship with Him that grew more intimate with each passing day. Walk with me, as I share the way that bond began, bloomed, and evolved. Through these events you will see how I was made aware of my importance to Him.

∗

I have known of God since I was a little girl. I received that gift from my Mom who had converted to Catholicism in her youth. Growing up in a less than perfect home, I watched her lean on her faith through many difficult circumstances.

It was no surprise when she insisted that we attend the neighborhood Catholic school. In those days, you were initiated into your relationship with the Lord through what I like to call the, "thunder and lightning" program. I wrongly believed that God was a larger than life being who constantly roamed about waiting for you to mess up so that He could scare you with His feared appearance and correction, in order to be sure you wouldn't do it again. We were terrified of Him and those in charge of the school liked it that way. Four more years of high school under similar belief systems, and my faith philosophy was doomed. Not because of who I believed in, but *who I believed He was.*

Many years later, after climbing mountains of life hurdles, He placed an amazing woman of God in my path. Deb loved the Lord with every ounce of her being. She was quiet and gentle. You would never have known about all her years of study. The warmth of her smile, the kindness in her voice, and the attention she gave to every detail of conversations, let you know she was unique and worthy of God's devotion and love.

Deb and I worked together for almost eight years. She helped me to discover who my Savior truly was, through the truth of His Word. She put to rest all the fear I had carried with me for years. The fear was a concrete wall locking me out of my intimate relationship with Jesus; the very thing I needed to walk through every moment of my life.

The saving grace of my life was the truth-based knowledge that Jesus desired to have a relationship with me. I'm not talking about a surface thing. This is far deeper than many people will allow themselves to experience in their lifetimes. Jesus expects us to be ourselves with Him, even when it's hard to be that way with ourselves. He longs to listen to our heart's cries and joys. He wants to be part of our decisions and anxieties. *He desires to be closer than a brother.* (Proverbs 18:24)

We are not in need of someone to speak for us or take our concerns to Him. That is our responsibility and over time, will become our joy.

I have shared during Womens' conferences that Jesus' phone line is never busy, He never puts you on hold, and you need NO reservations to have time with the Lover of Your Soul.

Some of my most cherished conversations with Him, have been in the most unique places and circumstances. There is no one better prepared to walk with you through each "life-happening."

There have been many times that I have run to the phone to call Deb or another friend, when I found myself in a frenzy and needed help. Often, those calls went unanswered, because He was teaching me He is the true answer to all my needs.

Like many, I too stacked letters and titles at the end of my name during my extensive career as an educator. It started with Bachelor of Science, Magna Cum Laude, minoring in Special Education, and trained in special theories and learning programs for special needs learners. I earned a Master's degree, became an Advanced Professional Educator, and wrote summer education programs. More than once, I was nominated for the Teacher of the Year award, won Baltimore County Chamber of Commerce Awards, and other parent or PTA (Parent Teacher Association) nominated awards.

I was the Co-Partner of a Women's Ministry group, composed worship songs, played the piano, led worship, wrote faith-based plays, and authored conference workshops. I became an animated colorful character that God created to help women release pain through humor.

I've taught countless groups of children about their amazing Jesus, the King of Kings. I have played characters in vacation bible school programs, ministry outreaches, and often ministered the Word to those at our church's homeless outreach.

At the time of this book's publishing, I will have added certified Christian Minister and Prayer Counselor to that list. My goal is to become a Christian Counselor and Pastor. He oversees that timeframe.

What will all of my titles and accomplishments mean when my time on the earth ends? What will I hear when I stand before His throne? Yes, many of those things were for His Kingdom and glory, but who am I to Him? What will He call me? What name will cause me to melt at His feet? He was already at work to answer my questions. Let's continue.

My bond with my Savior had been established. I was growing stronger as I became aware of His presence throughout the rough spots in my life. And yet, there was still a void within my soul. The unfulfilled yearnings I needed from my earthly father left me questioning my worth and importance to my heavenly Father. Who am I to Him? Recently, during a quiet time with Jesus, He led me to ponder another series of events in my life.

\*

I was first saved in 1995. My husband Tom and I had moved from Perry Hall, Maryland to New Freedom,

Pennsylvania, believing if we put distance between the earlier miscarriages and our new home, the pain would lessen and be easier to handle. A time of "new freedom" that we longed for and placed hope within.

But in Pennsylvania, it had happened again. In 1996, we were in the midst of dealing with our fifth miscarriage. While the circumstances again left us numb, we discovered, after the necessary surgery, that this baby saved my life because of where it was located. Had the pregnancy never occurred, I would have died from the problem that was discovered. Still reeling, I was already questioning why God would have allowed this to happen to us again.

Fortunately, He put an amazing Pastor and his wife literally in our backyard. They helped to dispel the ideas that God had allowed this to happen. They helped us to see that God Himself was weeping over this loss and our others. While it was still a new way of thinking for me, I decided to let God know I wanted proof it was Him.

I was sitting in the car waiting for Tom and I said quite arrogantly, "This better be You Lord, working in my life right now, or I am finished!"   Quietly, I heard, "Philippians 2:13."

I will admit that I was not a frequent bible reader. As much as I love to read, it wasn't a book that was known to me, even after twelve years of religious schooling.

So, when we got home, I opened the new bible we had been given by that same Pastor and his wife. Philippians 2:13 says, *"for it is God who works in you to will and to act in order to fulfill His good purpose."* People who know me, will tell you it's quite miraculous for me to be speechless - but I was. Tears streamed down my face and my soul knew who was speaking to me.

✳

In April of 2018, my dearest friend Deb, was called home to receive her crown of glory. While she had traveled a courageous road, believing God would heal her, it was in heaven that she became whole.

I was privileged to be part of a small group of sisters who went daily to help her with needs and pray over her for healing. I felt like a part of me was gone when she passed away. God had already told me it was time for He and I to continue the healing journey that had started with Deb at my side, so long ago.

A bond had developed between the small group of sisters (her handmaidens) and I felt that even though we had gone through the funeral together, we needed our own time of closure. So, a dinner and a time of fellowship was arranged for Deb's family and her handmaidens.

As I planned, I felt led to design a shirt in memory of Deb. She was so special to each of us. Purple was her favorite color and the color of royalty, as daughters of the King. She collected angels, and one was placed on the shirt with her name. Deb always wished everyone she encountered, Blessings! That wonderful word was added to one of the sleeves. There was one sleeve left. I decided to ask Kevin, her husband, which Bible verse was her favorite. At first, he sighed and said," Gosh, Michele, she had so many." I asked him to give it some thought and prayer. A few days later, I received a text message that simply said, Philippians 2:13. Undone, almost describes my reaction.

✳

In the last months, I have watched my strong, fear-less husband, battle the side effects of chemotherapy. The physical price of these effects is horrific and takes a toll on everyone in the circle of care. My knight, who fooled so many by his size compared to his strength, was fading before my eyes.

Throughout our entire lives we have tackled difficul-ties together or he has carried me through them, so you can imagine how difficult this is to watch. While we have managed to find things to laugh about and hold dear to our hearts, we have also had moments of conversation that shouldn't have to take place until at least ten years from now.

After one of the tougher nights, I decided to have a heart-to-heart talk with the Lord. I picked up Deb's pic-ture on the way to the living room as Tom lay sound asleep. There were puddles of tears, head shaking doubts, and comments sent angrily to heaven via the ceiling. I let Him know in no uncertain terms that this was too much to handle. I asked questions and pretty much demanded answers!

Most of all, I told Him that I couldn't handle this alone nor did I want to be left ALONE, again. This pain was too familiar. I had been here so many times before; as a child, in my youth, as an adult. No more, Lord! After a long while, and cried out, I gathered myself, put Deb's picture back in place, and was able to fall asleep next to my knight.

The next morning, I went through my usual morning routines and sat down to check my phone. Without thought, I opened my Bible app. and quickly scrolled to the verse of the day. My jaw dropped and my eyes froze, Philippians 2:13.

It took my breath away. God had heard my desperate cries and fears. He was letting me know I wasn't in this alone. He is always available to me and when it's time for my knight in shining armor to enter through the gates of heaven, I won't be alone, not as long as He is King of Kings and Lord of my life.

When it's my time to return home, I will melt at His feet when He looks into my eyes and says, "YOU ARE MINE!" For it is Him, my Father, who works in me, who pours His love over me, and delights in me as His own! I am a Daughter of the King!

*Psalm 27:4*
*One thing I ask from the Lord, and this only do I seek:*
*That I may dwell in the house of the Lord all the days of my*
*life, to gaze on the beauty of the Lord and to seek Him in*
*His temple.*

Other names God has given me:

- **Apple of His Eye**
- **Ambassador for Christ**
- **Rosa Joy Bloomington**
- **Teacher** (The Bible holds us more accountable)
- **Mighty Warrior**

- **Child of God**
- **Woman of the Word**

# FEARFULLY AND
# WONDERFULLY MADE

Psalm 139, verse 14 says, *"I praise you (Lord) because I am fearfully and wonderfully made, your works are wonderful, I know that full well.* In this verse, King David knew the Lord so well that he knew the Lord loved him and made him perfectly, just the way he was. This knowledge allowed King David to be happy with who he was.

There are many scriptures that describe how unique each of us are to the Lord. For some of us, it's easy to associate that pleasure with how we look to God. For others, it is foreign because of our inability to experience that warmth from our earthly parents, let alone our Heavenly Father.

If you allow yourself the vulnerability of seeing yourself as He sees you, you will discover God indeed has an individual fondness for you, despite how many children He calls His own.

For me, as with everything in my life, it was a process. It took a long time to allow myself to be me. One of my more time-consuming homework assignments from the early days of therapy, was to make hundreds of copies of the single sentence, "I deserve to be happy," and place them all over the house.

When people care deeply for us, they often give us an endearing name. A way of setting us apart as special to them. I remember the first time I received a special name from the Lord. One of the ladies I had met at our new church, came up to me after a service, and patted my shoulder. She said, "God says you are the apple of His eye!" Now many of you will say, "That's right from the Bible, anyone could be called that!" True, since you can find that verse in Deuteronomy 32:10. However, when the Lord wants you to know something, He sometimes has someone tell you. A special feeling envelopes you when you hear what He declares over you. It tells you it is truly from Him. There is no doubt it is meant for you!

I had never heard the verse quoted above. I didn't even take into consideration that I was a teacher and teachers were always associated with apples! I melted in the warmth of what was spoken to me. I had worth to my Maker! He had singled me out. I was undone!

✳

Years later, my husband Tom decided it was time for a new car for my travels to and from Baltimore each day. We loved our Subaru and ventured out to find a new one.

Following the lead of our credit union, we went to two dealers, Apple Subaru in York and a dealer in Baltimore. We had narrowed almost everything down and the dealers were close in the final cost of the cars we were considering. We just needed to pick the right dealer. Tom was scheduled to run ambulance that evening, so our search ended for the day as we headed home for him to prepare for his shift.

I looked out of the front window as he drove away and casually said aloud, "Lord, if we're supposed to buy the car from Apple, could you just put an apple in the sky?" I laughed as I went to change my clothes.

Nothing could have prepared me for what happened next. I returned to close the curtains at the front window. There, floating serenely across the sky in front of me, was a hot air balloon in the shape of an apple! I believe it was one of those moments when God said to Jesus, "Watch this!" I am sure that my reaction did not disappoint them!

After what seemed like forever, I ran to the phone and called Tom to share the news. "The car should come from Apple!" After a laughter filled explanation, he went back to his responsibilities.

The next morning, he arrived home with the Sunday paper that proudly displayed the Appleby Windows hot air balloon that had traveled across the area skies the previous day. Was that enough? Not for God!

At church, it was a weekend for armed services recognition and we had a guest speaker. We all stood and applauded to welcome him as our Pastor shared his name... General Applebaum! God's fingerprints were everywhere and He still wasn't finished.

God, once again, used pieces of my past to draw attention to the blessings He was pouring into our lives. My love of worshipping Him through song, created the necessary connections.

When my parents bought their first home in the country, the previous owners could not move an upright piano that was left in the basement. It became one of my favorite toys (I was 5), and it wasn't long before I was playing tunes by ear. Later, in my teens, my Mom found a lovely lady who gave piano lessons not far from our home. She signed me up and I walked to her house for my lessons.

I discovered rather quickly; the regimen needed for learning wasn't appealing to me at all! I much preferred the quiet contemplation of playing with the keys and discovering what would result.

Not long after I began the work of healing from difficulties, I was told that God was going to put the keys in my hands. The piano, once again, became a first aid kit for my soul during those tough times. Not only did God guide my hands on the keys, He gave me words that soothed my inner being and helped me to remember His goodness despite what I was experiencing. It was during this season; He gave me a simple song. Here's part of that song.

*Lord, You give good gifts to Your children,*
*Lord, You give good gifts to Your children,*
*Gifts from their Father above, wrapped in His love.*

*Ask for your gifts from your Father,*
*Ask for your gifts from your Father,*
*He'll give you them straight from His heart of love!*

Now, back to the car story. We were on our way to the Apple dealer to pick up our new car when God placed that song in my head again. I sang it aloud as I went to pick up Tom to go to the dealer.

When we arrived at Apple, our eyes scanned the lot for our new car. It was nowhere to be seen. That's odd we thought. Usually, they have them parked out front to be delivered. Filled with excitement, we went in and met with our salesman. After all of the paperwork was completed, he handed me my first remote key ring. Moving up, I thought!

Then, he began to explain its use. Following his instructions, I could hear the car responding by its beeps somewhere in the area. Tom and I both looked at each other wondering where it was. I finally said, "Where is the car? We didn't see it when we pulled in."

The salesman laughed and replied, "Oh, we place it on the showroom floor when we deliver a new vehicle. It is covered by a car cover and we unwrap it for the new owners, just a like a gift!" What can I say? Tom and I looked at each other and smiled ear to ear!

✳

Years later, God again carried me through some difficult events. This time He used Tom, my precious knight as His messenger to remind me of how special I am to Him.

A nasty fall in my classroom in 2016 led to issues that made it increasingly difficult for me to teach. We decided in 2017, that my career as an educator for thirty-eight and a half years needed to end. It was a difficult decision and I honestly believe God used the surgeries and therapy that took me out of the classroom to help me transition into not being there anymore.

Once again, Tom insisted the occasion be celebrated and remembered with a special piece of jewelry. Since we were in the midst of his first year of immunotherapy due to some skin cancer, I agreed we would do something special when the dust settled. While he was patient as the time passed, he never let me forget that we needed to celebrate.

After the events of this past year, he became more insistent we honor my career. His questions of, "What do you want?" and "When are we going?" became a daily part of our mornings.

Finally, we made our way to the jewelers and searched for the perfect keepsake.

Each sparkling case was carefully checked, and catalogs became the next place we perused. While ideas were shared and options explored, I wasn't quite sure what it would take to commemorate my professional career. Then, from across the store, one of the ladies who was helping us, motioned to me in that familiar teacher fashion, to come see what she had found.

It took my breath away! There it was--perfect-- just what God would have chosen for me and the perfect treasure Tom wanted to give me! He glowed to see me beam with joy over what was chosen.

I am fearfully and wonderfully made by my Heavenly Father who has fondly called me the "apple of His eye."

His choice for my soul mate gave me a precious treasure so I will never forget the name He gave me!

# TEARS OF A CLOWN

There are certain things we each search for during our time on earth. Some are innate and some grow out of what we strive to become. Regardless of their origin, every human, whether consciously or unconsciously, yearns for the prize at the end of each search.

I use the term prize loosely because, of course, not all searches end in joy or fulfillment. Sometimes there is an endpoint, a type of satisfaction, while others seem hollow or appear a failure, but the pursuit goes on.

There are some people who appear to be fulfilled and yet hidden deep inside them is an emptiness aching to be satisfied. The empty wells remain dry despite endless efforts to fill them with what they believe is water. Some of us grow up with these chasms deep inside.

People inadvertently believe the issues they grew up around are a direct result of something they caused or did not accomplish. Oftentimes, the people involved in the issues are so burdened by the situations themselves, they fail to realize their impact on others. Sadly, others do, yet have no regard for the fallout.

There are those who sacrifice themselves to meet the

needs of everyone else. Others won't spend the energy or the effort, assign the blame outside of their responsibilities, and walk away.

If any of these thoughts are connecting with you on some level, realize you are not alone. One of the hardest prisons I had to work hard to escape from, was the realization that my struggles were not unique to me.

You see, when the enemy convinces you that you are the only one experiencing a problem, he has you captive. He convinces you to not share or speak about your anxieties, or you will be the outcast. He is without a doubt, the father of lies. Your silence keeps you in prison. I was tortured by the silence of two men in my life. I longed for understanding, affection, and validation from both, but neither of them respected me enough to satisfy that yearning. Unfortunately, for too long, I believed their silence was a result of something I caused, so I deserved the consequence. Another lie.

God emphatically instructed me to tell His women not to remain silent. The captive audience we supply the enemy in silence, is unmistakable evidence of its dangers and why God is determined for us to claim victory over it. The Word states that Jesus came so that we could each be FREE! I was blessed when I found refuge in a dear, trusted friend, Deb.

*A word of caution: Pray and ask the Lord who you should confide in when you have an issue. You need a TRUSTED confidant when you are struggling with issues that can be larger than yourself. There may be more than one conversation that is needed to move you to victory, so you need Him to guide you to His choice for support.*

\*

Growing up, I helped with the responsibilities of caring for two younger brothers and other household duties. My mom suffered with a multitude of illnesses. Whether consciously or not, I believe my father felt like her problems began because of my birth. I discovered later on that he was also disappointed I was a girl. As the oldest, I tried hard for a long time to help her get things done. While she was grateful and the efforts were noteworthy, I was still a child trying to measure up to an adult's ability.

The result for me was never receiving the attention/ approval I craved from my other parent. I am not assigning guilt here in any way. They were suffering with their own issues.

I grew up needing and craving attention and affection. This was compounded by the fact that my ideas of how to attain them were skewed by my circumstances. So, I did what I knew to do; I was a helper, a fixer, a rescuer. As time went on, those skills wore thin, and the social demands of growing up became more challenging. Those abilities were no longer a valued commodity.

That's when I discovered I could make people laugh. It started as attempts to cover up things I didn't know much about or was uncomfortable trying. It was easier to joke about them than to fail miserably at the mercy of the people with whom I was desperately trying to fit in with or become friends.

One of the stories my students loved to hear, was my first ski trip with the Girl Scouts. I was terrified. Putting any moveable objects beneath my feet was a critical mistake. After getting all the equipment on, we inched our way up to the area where we would get our free lesson. I stayed far back in the line of trainees and watched in distress as each person took their turn gliding down to the instructor.

My turn came. It seemed like forever until I was standing at the top of the tiny hill facing the instructor at the bottom. With much encouragement, I dug the poles in and pushed off. The movement downward surprised me completely, and I lost sight of the instructor or how to stop when reaching him. At the last minute, I saw him approaching at what seemed like lightning speed. I started screaming, "Move! Move!" His calm response was "Turn your skis!" He never finished the second request because I ran right over him in a white cloud. Everyone in the area rolled in laughter. To hide my disgrace, I stood up and raised my arms in victory. Everyone cheered!

I spent the rest of the day in the ski lodge drinking hot chocolate and laughing at everyone else on the slopes. But I felt like a failure and alone.

I got the attention of others, but never learned what I really needed to be one of them. I lived in constant anxiety of whether they would continue to include me, or toss me to the side. I settled for the laughter they rewarded me with, but when I was alone, I experienced the "tears of a clown." The facial expressions I displayed gave no indication of how desperate I was to feel valued by others. I ached to be automatically included in gatherings or events without a second thought or after others were chosen. How I longed to be the one who others waited for as I picked my camping tent mate or chemistry partner. I spent nights when dances occurred at high school, home by myself contemplating through tears how it would have felt to be desired enough to have received an invitation. I was mesmerized by what each passing moment of those events must have been like.

It wasn't until I met Tom, I truly began to discover and enjoy laughing for the pleasure it gave. It didn't take him long to see beneath my tired smile. He used our time together to help me learn to count on him. I began to believe he wouldn't abandon me without explanation.

With each hurdle we cleared, he valued me in a deeper way and poured his love selflessly over me. He once told me that he had decided, "It was time for the rescuer to be rescued." He waited, while I grew the courage to trust him. I questioned him often about why he loved me. I couldn't understand why he could, when others I gave my heart to didn't, or used it for their own purposes. While his response correctly declared it was their loss, I continued to search for what was missing in me that would have delivered what I so desperately wanted. He was my best friend before he became my true love!

On our wedding day, it was as if we stood on the top of the highest mountain, celebrating the beginning of new hopes and dreams together. Our hearts were overflowing, what a glorious beginning! So many guests shared with us that our faces were glowing with love for one another that day.

Those precious investments in the earlier days, would

become the strength we would draw from in later years. The whole first year of our marriage, we played pranks on each other. Every day, whoever arrived home first, had one planned for the other. He was always better at 'one upping' me. I'm surprised our neighbors didn't complain about our screaming and laughing. What wonderful memories!

\*

Laughter was an integral part of my classroom, as well. Smiles were required each morning and during class rotations. There were many kiddos who thought they could outlast me by not smiling. The simple pleasure of a smile should never be overlooked.

I had the reputation as the prankster of the building. No one was off limits. I was once caught by a substitute principal in a squirt bottle battle with a fellow teacher across the hall. How the kids cherished that moment and so many more. There were school supplies that dangled from our classroom ceiling and sometimes flew out the window. The joy was contagious as one of my classes began to bring their math teachers supplies back to our homeroom and hide them from him.

My pranks reached beyond the current students I taught. Students who were in fourth or fifth grade were never off limits until they graduated to middle school. One fourth grader arrived at his cubby to gather his things for afternoon classes only to find it completely empty. He knew exactly where to locate them as he raced into my room with a huge smile. More than once, prior students would turn to find me sitting next to them in one of their classes. Their reactions and remarks of, "Uh oh!" were priceless. I still smile remembering a young man who engaged in a prank war with me because he had not been placed in my class. He arrived back in his homeroom one morning after library to find his entire desk and chair completely wrapped in cellophane! More than one class enlisted the help of other teachers and administrators, to out prank me. A grade level partner and I had a challenging time shuffling her students across the hall to her room each morning in time for announcements because they loved to visit. My high reach grabber became my imaginary chihuahua in an attempt to bark and nip at their heels ushering them across the hall. This clever group recruited the principal to visit my classroom at dismissal one afternoon to investigate my having a pet in the building. She arrived with the entire class behind her. A teacher in trouble with the principal for breaking school rules. What amazing moments to look back upon.

My goal, while at school, was to rewrite the fear that I had grown up with as a child. I worked to replace it with a desire for my students to want to be at school and learn in a nurturing environment. I aimed for them to become driven lifetime learners, not just students for one year. More than one parent asked for my help in convincing their sick child to stay at home until they were better.

My last class kept me on my toes. They were quite clever at making the best of opportunities to keep the challenge going between students and teacher. They also had the benefit of their siblings who had passed through my doors before them, and delighted in helping them. I enjoyed just as many previous students visiting me at the beginning of a new year, as my newest arrivals!

One morning as the teachers were stationed in the hall during class rotations, my cherubs decided to lock me out of the classroom. While I never saw it coming, I had a key and the door was quickly unlocked. They, however, were waiting on the other side and pushed it closed, relocking it. After several tries and tons of giggles, I called into the room using the intercom phone. My request was met with louder laughter, but the door was opened. After a brief discussion on the safety involved with my being out of the room, we got to work. As I thought about their win, I just couldn't let it go and announced after lunch that the assistant principal would be visiting us to discuss the incident and safety concerns. What they didn't know, was while they were at lunch, I had shared their victory prank with the secretaries. I enlisted their help to call our room at dismissal and share that the assistant principal wouldn't be able to stop by. My "Gotcha!" and their response were worthy of an Emmy. The very next morning, several of them spoke to the secretaries on their way into school and asked for their help to plan their retribution. Several days later, one secretary called into our room in the morning and announced the meeting I had missed before school with the assistant principal would have to be rescheduled. He was requesting I stop by his office to take care of this task. I was dumbfounded and completely unaware of any meeting that morning. It was completely out of character for me to miss one. As I shared these thoughts aloud, the grins on my students' faces grew wider and wider. I made the mistake of saying, "What are you smiling about?" Their chorus of, "Gotcha!" was priceless.

*

Did you know that God laughs in heaven? It's true.

I genuinely believe He has a sense of humor, (I have seen Him use a roll of toilet paper to minister to a dear sister.) He's not playing a joke on anyone in these verses below. God laughs at His enemies! Consider the power of that.

*"The One enthroned in heaven laughs; the Lord scoffs at them." Psalm 2:4*

*"The wicked plot against the righteous and gnash their teeth at them; but the Lord laughs at the wicked, for He knows their day is coming." Psalm 37:12-13*

*"But You laugh at them, Lord; you scoff at all those nations." Psalm 59:8*

There are countless ways laughter heals, cleanses, revives, and even improves mental health. These come as no surprise to the Lord! He created laughter. He knows how much His children need to release the pressures of life through a good, long, rib-aching laugh. He also wants us to remember the verse that declares, *"If God is for us, who can be against us?" Romans 8:31.*

So, when those wicked past issues raise their nasty heads against you, remember to Whom you belong. Place them in the hands of the Master, crawl up into His lap, and have a good hardy laugh with Him!

Finally, make sure to look for opportunities to laugh. They're all around you. They have a time and a place. Most have a healthy purpose; to bring joy and create memories.

Tom and I still play jokes on each other and laugh at ones that hold such fond memories. We recently had to wait for over an hour for our oncologist in an exam room. Tom is not good at waiting in the doctor's office; good teachers are born that way. When forty-five minutes had passed, he announced he was heading to the restroom. He opened the door and asked the nurse where it was. As he headed back to the room, I heard him chat with the nurse about how busy the doctor must have been. When he opened the door, I burst into laughter. He thought I did because he asked about the doctor and I knew he was impatient. What he didn't know, was that when he had washed his hands the water faucet in the sink sprayed the lower half of his shirt. It looked like it was water tye-dyed! When he discovered it, we rolled in laughter together!

As I wrote this pondering, I asked Tom about one favorite prank he had pulled on me. He chose one that he ingeniously planned during our first year of marriage. Our bedroom was quite spacious and included a half-bath in the far corner of the room. One night as we were finishing our good night conversation, he got up to use the restroom. It was his habit to leave the door a bit ajar, so I waited for him with my back to the bathroom door. After a few minutes, I turned over to check and saw that the door was still ajar. With little thought, I turned back on my side. About thirty seconds later, he rose on my side of the bed and let out a chilling roar! I came up and off the bed, bounced against the headboard, and rolled off his side of the bed, to the floor! He couldn't get off the floor for at least twenty minutes. He had crawled all the way from the bathroom and across the floor, leaving the door ajar. After catching my breath, I laughed as I watched him from under the bed rolling in victory!

Not to be outdone, I would like to share one of which I am quite proud! Tom used to work from eleven at night until seven in the morning. He is still getting used to sleeping during the time he used to work, and many times, stays up later watching television. One night, I lay in bed just thinking about the day's events when I realized he was listening to a show on UFOs. After about twenty minutes or so, I heard him go into the kitchen. I could tell that he had grabbed a snack and was probably watching the show from the dining room table. I giggled as I contemplated my next moves. Our kitchen and dining room were newly remodeled. One of the dining room fan/light switches is in our main hallway. It came equipped with a dimmer. I peeked out of the bedroom door and down the hall. Sure enough, there was a glow from the dining room light. That set my plan in motion. Without a sound, I traveled down the hall to the wall plate that controlled the dining room light. Very gently, I touched the dimmer and the light in the room dimmed and then returned to its original strength. I almost lost it as I often do when I try to pull a first-rate prank. There was no sound in the dining room. The chewing stopped. So, I decided to go for the win. Once more, the light dimmed and went back to normal. Then, I heard his chair roll backward. He came around the corner like a deer in headlights. I slid down the wall in hysterics! He didn't even offer to help me to get up!

Treat yourself and those you love to a good laugh often. Life is hard enough and without a good, healthy, relief valve, days will only seem tougher.

Just like those accounts of God's faithfulness that are so valuable when you wonder if He hears at all, memories of shared laughter will help to carry you through moments that seem without relief or end. Laugh- it's good for you!

# WILL

Consider this: How many times a day do you make choices in your life based on what you want or desire? Do you consider what affect your decisions will have on others?

How willing are you to bend or make sacrifices because you know someone else's desire differs from yours? How many times have you willingly given up your time to do something that you know means so much to someone else?

In the garden before He was arrested, Jesus said, *"Father, if you are willing, take this cup from Me; yet not My will, but Yours be done."* (Luke 22:42) That moment in Scripture has been repeated millions of times. When we say the Lord's prayer we affirm, *Your kingdom come, Your will be done, on earth as it is in heaven."* (Matthew 6:10) And yet the true power behind this moment, when Jesus gave Himself into His Father's hands and will, is much deeper than this.

Remember, that Jesus is our intercessor at the right hand of the Father. He has experienced every single thought, feeling, emotion, pain, frustration, etc. that we experience as His children. Which means He was also tempted by the same day-to-day life struggles we experience and oftentimes fail at overcoming. He never lost sight of what His Father's will was for His life. He never put off something He knew His Father needed Him to do at a determined moment. He continually put aside His desires and will and gave Himself to what was required by His Father.

As my husband's caregiver, I take the moments I can, while he rests, to just sit on the deck and open my heart to the Lord. Just recently, He allowed me to see how much Jesus gave for me and my future eternity in heaven.

It wasn't just that moment in Gethsemane that Jesus surrendered His will to the Father. It was the culmination of His surrender which took Him to the Cross and placed Him at the right hand of His Father.

Being a caregiver gives you a new perspective that helps you appreciate the sacrifices Jesus continually made. And just as caregivers give their all to their loved ones and often still fall short, each of us would be facing that eternal shortfall had it not been for Jesus and the surrender of His will.

**Try this.** Spend at least one day making all your decisions based on what one other person would want instead of you. Pay close attention to your thoughts and feelings as time goes by. Does it get easier or more difficult to make those choices?

**Up for a bigger challenge?** Try the same activity for someone who is not one of your favorite people! Compare the amount of time you are still willing to give up your will and the amount of inner strength it takes.

# ILLNESS AND LOSS

In 2002, we purchased a home in Hanover, PA, so we could be closer to our church. For many years, my husband Tom had operated a successful lawn and landscaping business, in addition to his full-time job, and now offered to take care of the church grounds every week. Moving to Hanover, allowed him to trim away two and a half hours of travel time on the Saturdays that he took care of the church grounds for seven to eight hours. The move allowed me to become more involved in children's ministries and furthered my desire to become a Pastor through the study of God's Word.

When we purchased our home, the previous owner shared that her husband had died the year before. Even though he had done everything imaginable to prepare the home so that she would be able to handle its maintenance, she could no longer bear to live there. She said, "You know who your true friends are when an illness strikes."

I learned what she meant in 2015 when Tom was diagnosed with malignant melanoma. It was as if someone had pulled the rug out from under our lives. We were instantly in a whirlwind of uncertainty and disbelief. There were times I felt like it was impossible to breathe.

As we began this journey, I remembered those words and found that we were indeed surrounded by people who loved us and were willing to walk beside us. Not only family, but dear friends, and even the parent of one of my students! My team-teaching partner took my phone call on the evening we learned of Tom's diagnosis and made sure that my students were taken care of each day while I found the ground again.

The specialists God put in our path were amazing and treated us as if we were their only patients. Before the end of 2017, Tom had experienced two reoccurrences and was classified as Stage 4. Once again, God intervened and showed our amazing oncologist a path of immuno-therapy to use. This yearly treatment bought Tom two years in remission.

We had just celebrated his 62$^{nd}$ birthday and two-year remission anniversary, when a new problem appeared on his eyelid. Having three doctors examine the eyelid and decide it was not a melanoma presentation was a comfort. However, it still had to be removed, and when it was, we were devastated to learn it had tiny melanoma cells on a small piece of skin next to it. Two more tiny sites were discovered along with the report that not all of the affected eyelid had been removed successfully.

Once again, our oncologist looked for another path that would not result in Tom losing the rest of his eyelid. And this is where we are today; fighting with oral chemo-therapy to regain remission.

After five years with our amazing God provided oncologist, we were dealt another blow. He himself was diagnosed with an exceedingly rare form of cancer and had to close his practice. While we continue to have an amazing team of providers, he was the captain of the ship, and we felt his and his staff's loss in so many ways.

I was prompted to share all of these stories, because we had been so blessed with providers and staff members who treated us as family, not just patients. It was difficult to have to step outside of that security to deal with other health care providers who are part of a huge medical system or just consider what they do, as a job.

Patients are not numbers, but human beings, who receive life changing diagnoses. They need time to process what is happening and how to handle the circumstances. Many times, these health care workers refuse to see that the manner in which they handle people, can determine how people handle their illness or the procedures that are suggested to them. A positive experience where a patient is respected and valued makes their path and that of their loved ones easier to walk.

As time goes on, and you continue the battle, it's often true that your journey-mates disappear. Surprisingly, the people you were sure you could count on, aren't anywhere to be found. Then, there are the precious gems God puts in your path who come right alongside and find countless ways to help you through. We have been abundantly blessed by the things people have offered to help us to accomplish. Our own band of Prayer Warriors lift us before the throne regularly! We have also learned it's so much healthier to regard the glass as half full and not half empty.

One last thought; no one is ever sure of what to say when life deals tragic blows to those we know or love. The worst thing to do, is to say nothing. Loss of any kind is difficult. Many times, people are numb to what is happening around them. It's okay to be at a loss for the right thing to say. But staying away and saying nothing, conveys something entirely different to those in pain. Sitting silently with them speaks volumes.

Tom and I will be greeted by five beautiful angels when we arrive in heaven. While we were not able to enjoy them here with us on Earth because of the miscarriages, we will have eternity to spend with them in heaven.

Thirty- five years ago, when our problems started, I could never have seen the circumstances this way. What I do remember, is that so many people said nothing, just a timid smile shared in passing. That wasn't a comfort; it was perceived as a lack of concern or compassion. They didn't mean either, but, at the time, I was sure they did! Take the time to pray before you meet with someone who has experienced great illness or loss. God is well-versed in what to say or do. Many times, I have asked His words become mine, so there are no missteps.

Finally, don't be surprised when He puts people in your path who are experiencing the same pain you have come through, because He will. You will be equally surprised at how much further you heal, when you help another hurting soul.

I had a dear friend in our Women's Ministry who used to tell me, "Don't waste the pain," as I walked through each miscarriage. The only thing I didn't want to waste, was the time it would have taken for me to put my hands around her neck and violently shake her! I was a volcano of bitterness and disappointment.

Years later, the Lord had me create and teach a workshop on the Seven Keys of Healing. I was so excited to share what He laid on my heart.

The session began and we were rolling. As we discussed each new key, I shared how they had helped me in my journey of healing, from losing our babies.

Then, from the back of the room a woman began to wail in pain. Her agony could be felt by every woman there. Some began to cry, some prayed, and those with her got down on the floor and tried to console her. It sounded like the wailing that must have taken place when Herod the Great ordered the killing of all the male babies in order to try to kill baby Jesus.

As time passed, the room emptied until it was just the woman, her family, and myself. When she was able to stand, she took me in her arms and held tight. She thanked me for having the courage to share my pain. Within that moment, she was able to get hold of the agony of her stillborn son, and finally release what had been pent up within her for weeks. Her healing had begun.

Amid the last few weeks of working on this pondering, I received an interesting picture of these kinds of circumstances. Moving through an illness with medical providers can look and feel different. Tom and I have had to work with many of those described below. My hope is that if you must walk through your own illness experience, it will be dotted with those in the last group.

1.  There are those who you reach out to in a health cri-

sis who point to the twelve-foot fence you must get over. They never look up from the pile of paperwork they are inundated with on their desk. You might get a quick smile as you move along.

2. There are those who not only point to the fence, they walk you halfway and get distracted, leaving you alone to finish the walk. You might get a quick glance back to be sure you're still moving in the right direction.

3. There are those who walk you all the way to the fence and hope you can get over it. They're off to the next item on their to-do list.

4. The last group of people not only point out the path and walk you to the fence, they use their knowledge and expertise to help you get over the fence successfully. And if that's not enough, they've already planned for someone to be waiting on the other side of the fence to take you to the next stop on your journey.

Something to ponder: Which group will you fit in if an illness knocks on the door of someone in your life?

# A GLIMPSE OF THE UNSEEN

Over the years, I have heard many Pastors share that people who think it is all right to arrive at church after worship, are making a huge mistake. Many people believe that hearing the Word of God is the essence of the service. While it holds monumental significance, the preparation of a believer's heart for that deposit of the Word occurs during worship. The fresh fertile ground of the heart is ready for what God will speak to His people!

Additionally, Psalm 22 verse 3 gives us an important purpose for praise and worship: "*God inhabits the praises of His people.*" *(KJV)* He dwells within them, and prepares to bless the poured-out hearts of those who love Him!

So, if you believe that you're not missing much by arriving after worship, you are really cheating yourself out of an intimate time with Jesus! He taught me a valuable lesson about the importance He places on worship and its significance between Him and His believers.

*

The planning of a women's retreat begins long before

there is any outward sign of the event. Most are birthed out of a season of prayer or the laying of a burden on the hearts of those who serve the Lord. Each detail is bathed in prayer and fine-tuned, by the guiding hand of the Holy Spirit.

Key components of the event like location, guest speakers, and who will lead worship are most often decided early in the process. I remember vividly as we planned an annual retreat, the worry that began to grow within the leader of our group, when a worship team seemed nowhere to be found.

After times of prayer about the issue, she called and asked if I would plan and lead worship for the event. For you to fully understand my reaction, I should share that at my one and only piano recital, I shook from head-to-toe and couldn't for the life of me remember what note the first piece began with! "Are you sure?" I asked. She was, and shared the Lord had made it clear to her that I had received His nod.

Ecstasy and terror took turns within my heart each day as I planned for this honor. I practiced day and night, even taking my music to school and playing a piano in a storage closet during lunch times to get it right.

As the plans came together, I became confident the songs the Lord had laid on my heart, were indeed the right ones. He even gave me another original song that touched the hearts of many that day.

What wasn't growing stronger, was my belief in my own ability to lead without making mistakes. When playing for myself or for my husband Tom, it was less painful to make a mistake, stop, and pick up again. When leading others, the ability to begin again, wasn't an option.

The day came when we headed down to the church in Baltimore for the rehearsal and preparation. When we got to the neighborhood, I was shocked to discover that it was in an all-residential section.

We pulled up to the curb in front of the church. There it was, smack dab in the middle of a group of closely placed, older homes. If we hadn't stopped, I would never have known that it was a church!

I was not impressed. Not that I had to be impressed. But I just had this grandiose vision of what the church would look like and this picture didn't even come close! A simple older building with stained-glass windows. My next thought was even worse. "If this is what the outside looks like, I bet the piano is old and out-of-tune!"

As we entered the foyer, we climbed the short staircase and went through the double doors to the sanctuary. This had to be one of those moments when Jesus leaned forward on His throne next to His Father and said, "Watch her reaction now!"

There it was, in its elegance, sitting on the right-hand side of the altar. A beautiful, baby grand piano! I couldn't move for a few minutes because I just had to take it all in and glow with anticipation!

I timidly walked up to it and touched the keys, as if they would break, if my touch were too heavy. God had given me a grandiose instrument to lead His women into His presence!

I don't remember much of what happened that evening because I spent the whole evening at the keyboard. People will tell you that there is a distinct difference in the feel of different keyboards. Some are easy to adjust to, some are not. This keyboard felt as if it had been created for my fingers. They glided over the keys and it took little pressure to create the music that had been planned.

What an evening we had together; the Lord watching me play, just for Him, and me delighting in the pleasure of playing and singing for my King! That evening, I learned not to doubt what God has prepared for you when He asks you to honor His request.

As in many times before, God wasn't quite finished. Since we all lived in Pennsylvania, we had to leave for Baltimore very early the next morning. We planned to be at the church long before the ladies were to arrive.

As I drove to the park and ride, I prayed for peace, guidance, and a settled spirit. Then, quite surprisingly I heard myself say, "Lord, where my eyes fail at reading the music, let Your eyes take over. Where my hands fail at playing the right notes, let Your hands take over." I thought it was a cool addition to the prayer, but didn't think any more about it.

At the church, everyone busied themselves to prepare for a day of God's goodness. I panicked just a bit when I sat down at the keyboard to begin warming up and noticed that my hands were trembling. "Oh, no!" I thought. "I can't start this way!" I closed my eyes and pictured Him as an audience of one. Song by song, I practiced. Little by little, after correcting missteps, I felt increasingly comfortable with how each sounded.

It was a blessing to me that one of the ladies in the ministry was walking the sanctuary praying for the ladies who would be attending- preparing the atmosphere for

God and His goodness!

The beginning of this retreat was unique. We had the ladies walk into the sanctuary at the start of a song, and shared that they had each been invited to this event by the King Himself. It was exciting and powerful! I couldn't resist and looked up to see their faces. They were beaming with glory! Unfortunately, that's when I made my first mistake at the keys. I was shocked at how easily I recovered, but then I clearly heard the Holy Spirit say, "Keep your eyes on the music and keys."

Now if you've dealt with children at any time in your life, you will surely understand their almost innate instinct to push that "Don't!" envelope at least once. It almost always ends in a poor outcome.

The hard work and desire to please Jesus was blessing those in attendance. I was increasingly relaxed with each song. Then, the little kid in me once again, couldn't resist. I had to look out over the ladies again. When I did, my fingers landed in the wrong places once again. "Oh, Lord, I'm sorry!" It raced through my head. I found the right placement and went on.

The retreat ended as they all did, with the attendees not wanting to leave, and begging to know when we would be presenting the next event. We were exhausted, but full to the brim with gratitude to God for what He had allowed us to do for Him. It was a tradition for us to share a meal together before we headed home after each retreat.

As we traveled, the leader of the ministry started to ask each of us what we had seen God do that day; either in the lives of one of the attendees or our own. One by one we shared.

When it was my turn, I decided to share how anxious I had been about not making mistakes as I played. It was almost coming true when I warmed up and made errors. Then, I had to see the reaction of the ladies which caused me to miss a chord. I didn't listen when God told me not to take my eyes off the music or the keys, and goofed again, I admitted.

There was quiet in the van, and then the lady who had been praying in the church turned and said to me, "Michele, you didn't make any mistakes this morning. I was listening and I didn't hear a single mistake." This was agreed upon by others in the van who said the same things about the songs throughout worship. "There weren't any mistakes," they agreed. I smiled and thought they were being kind, because I guess they knew I was a little ashamed of myself.

But then I remembered the prayer from the morning.

"Lord, where my eyes fail at reading the music, let Your eyes take over. Where my hands fail at playing the right notes, let Your hands take over."

He had answered that prayer.

That wasn't all. He had protected me from what I had feared the most, while still teaching me a valuable lesson. He had honored my obedience to honor Him! What an amazing Father!

# IT'S ALL IN THE TIMING!

In the pastoral comedy, As You Like It, Shakespeare wrote, "All the world is a stage."

So true! Life is acted out day in and day out. Some actions deliberately planned, and others resulting from what seems like no direct influence. The acts go on continually, and the actors play well-learned parts, with little to no modifications. Most of the actors involved are self-serving in their roles. Sadly, more often than not, there seems to be no true purpose for each act, unless it's simply making it through another day or for personal gains.

We are a society of schedules, appointments, routines, and demands that leave little room for alterations. As a result, professions of, "I've got no time for the Lord", or serving Him to reach others, are commonplace. Fortunately, for every one of us, including those without the time, we are a priority to Him. His actions are deliberately orchestrated to draw us closer and bless us. (2 Peter 3:9 and Matthew 18:12-13)

As you will see in the following story, God used my faith, in its early stages, and the secret desires of my heart, to create a pathway for hurting souls to find Him. Despite the demanding requirements of a teaching career and the needs of our family, I found it pure joy to serve Him to reach others.

*

From childhood, I loved being on stage. I dreamed of being an actress, in the spotlight, letting the feelings deep within my heart be poured out with purpose. I remember when my Mom took my brother and I to appear on the television show 'Romper Room,' with Miss Sally. I was in my glory. They asked her to bring us back for another taping!

I spent countless moments in my room pretending to be someone from television, moving through their motions with delight. I sang song after song, emptying my heart to the silent applause of an adoring audience.

When God presented me with the persona of Rosa, I was ready to take on that challenge and give it my all. Rosa Joy Bloomington was born during the conference plans of a spring event. It was the first time I was asked to be the main speaker of a retreat. The focus of the event was the new growth the world enjoys each spring. We focused on life in the garden. The Holy Spirit gave me her name, at first, only as Rosa Bloomington. Rosa for roses and Bloomington because there are a ton of things blooming in spring. As she evolved, her costumes, props, and persona became more and more flamboyant. She wore her heart on her sleeve and had a childlike innocence that made it easy to feel as if you had known her forever.

God and I created a presentation in which the audience watched the evolution of Rosa Bloomington. God masterfully revealed how the disguises she wore in her life were peeled away to reveal a new creation. Piece by piece, the outrageous outfit became a beautiful white gown as she stood before Jesus to celebrate all He had done to heal her past. It was a spiritual birthday of sorts for me. He was detailing what the desired outcome was of the assignment He was giving me. In His precious loving way, He was proving to me I was qualified for the job through the realization of His work in my own life. While I worked diligently to minister to those in attendance, I was humbled as I felt Him minister to me in such a deep measure.

Providing an avenue for laughter was second nature to me. I spent many hours watching world-renowned comedians, to learn about timing and delivery. It took a while for me to be able to concentrate when first watching Carol Burnett and Tim Conway. I think they are my all-time favorites, (although I've watched many more)! Learning how to read your audience and anticipate reactions was easier because of my years in the classroom. I learned how to draw upon unexpected events to continue in the rhythm and enhance a performance.

We worked together, God and I, to offer a new path to broken souls for healing and restoration. His plans began in my head and heart just like the tiny bubbles you see at the bottom of a pot of water as it starts to boil. As time went by, the bubbles increased in size and movement. The excitement would build and I often laughed aloud, at the snippets of action that rolled through my mind.

Then, at a divinely timed moment, His Spirit moved within my heart and I knew it was time to sit down at the computer and begin writing. Our creation would pour out onto the pages and sometimes, my fingers could barely keep up with its flow. It was an amazing adrenaline rush and I've never tired of these intimate exchanges!

I am a lover of words, have written poetry and stories all my life. My students would always wait for rhyming thoughts or a silly pun sprinkled throughout the day. We loved word play!

We used word play so much for Rosa's performances and it was through her innocent misunderstandings that so many women could relate to her. Rosa was married to Bud Bloomington, and there were many references to their life together that ministered directly into the hearts of conference attendees. The Lord had fun with Rosa during those events, as well. Unplanned moments always seem to pop up and Rosa found herself on the opposite side of the fence. God is so good!

I feel led to share one specific event with you. When Rosa was in her infant stages, God supplied all that I needed to write the script, prepare her costume, create the props, and orchestrate the delivery. As time went on, He still gave me key pieces of what He wanted presented, however, sometimes it took longer for those pieces to 'arrive' so to speak. He was teaching me, through Rosa, to depend on Him and in His timing.

Then, came the 'test' of trust.

The latest conference plans were moving along and everything was put in place. Rosa, of course, would have her time slot as always. However, I hadn't heard from

God about His plan for her entrance and time was growing short. He had only given me bare bone thoughts on how Rosa was to interact throughout the day.

Now, I could have run off on my own and put something together. To be honest, I did consider that as we came down to one week before the conference. But even then, nothing came. I knew it was futile to act without God's leading. I would never accomplish what He had planned without Him.

The morning of the conference arrived and still no word. I dressed in the outrageous outfit as usual and paced, while the anxiety mounted within me. The women were arriving and I waited before taking my place in the foyer, to prepare for my entrance.

Silently, I held on, and listened for that still small voice. As I stood outside the sanctuary doors, I motioned for one of the girls in our ministry, to bring me her cell phone. She handed it to me within seconds of my scheduled entrance!

As always, Rosa's entrance was greeted with cheers and nervous anticipation. Her dialogue, that was unknown until seconds before, brought laughter and a unity in spirit that set the atmosphere for the day.

God taught me valuable lessons that day and, in the time, beforehand. He was aware of my need to know what to do, through Rosa, and its divine delivery would arrive at its appointed moment. He also wanted me to realize that I understood a piece of His heart, as we had planned so many events before. I knew, my God-given purpose, and knew it was dependent on Him. Finally, I learned to 'trust' His timing. There are no mistakes, with the King of Kings.

God's fingerprints on your life are distinct. No one else will be ministered to in the same way that God interacts with you. That can be a mountain for some people to get over or around, but it's true! It really shouldn't come as a surprise as His word tells us that He knows the number of hairs on our heads. (Luke 12:7)

My ponderings will not be the same as yours, nor should they. They are also dependent upon how intimate your relationship is with the Lord. God has used the unique outpourings of my heart and prayers and responded to them in language and actions that only I would recognize.

The Bible tells us that God is no respecter of persons. (Acts 10: 34-35) That means He loves you just as much as He loves me. He is ready and willing to meet you in ways that are just as extraordinary as you!

\*

Up for another example of timing and delivery?

When my brothers and I were growing up, we went to a popular spot for some summer vacations. Ocean City was a great family-oriented spot, where days were spent on the beach and nights on the boardwalk. During one summer, my parents took us off the beaten path to a place called, Frontier Town. It was an amusement like facility complete with a wild west main street, a cowboy gun battle, and a small Indian settlement. Families could take train rides and were stopped by robbers who took the bank delivery that the train carried.

I should also mention before continuing, that my Mom's heritage includes a Cherokee background. I spent most of my days wearing braids on both sides of my head to keep my long hair in place.

We made our way up and down the main street storefronts, had lunch in the saloon, and headed out to take a train ride. We had to pass the Indian settlement to get there.

As we approached, a young boy in the settlement about my age spotted me coming. Almost immediately, he started running in my direction. My family stopped and my eyes met his. While no one else in the family did an about face and started running, I did! He was in hot pursuit behind me! There was dust stirring as we covered the alleys between buildings and down main street.

The Indian parents and my own were having a wonderful time laughing at the 'cuteness' of the event. I was not humored! He was finally called off by his father and apologized for chasing a 'cute squaw.' I still was not humored!

At one point of my time with a particular ministry, we were invited to New York to present a conference. I was still learning the ropes and also dealing with memories that needed to be overcome. I was honored to be asked to join the small group that had been chosen to represent this ministry.

We had a wonderful drive and I saw parts of this beautiful country I had never enjoyed. We stayed at the Pastor's home and were treated with so many gestures of love.

The morning of the conference arrived and we prepared for the day ahead. As the service began, the worship band introduced a song that had been so powerful in their meetings over recent weeks. They shared they felt led to play it again by the leading of the Holy Spirit.

I don't remember much of what happened in worship after they played that song, because it touched me at my deepest core. It was written by an American Indian, Jonathan Maracle. It is called, <u>Rise Up Mighty Warrior.</u> If you have a background of things that you have believed in that were not correct, or been hurt often by others, this is a song for you. I strongly suggest you listen to it.

While it may or may not minister to you, it unraveled me until my soul was laid open. God was acknowledging the pains of my past and directing me to rise up and above them. It was almost as if He was giving me my marching orders for the next season of my life. He knew how much music and the words within songs spoke to my spirit and divinely prepared the timing of my own deliverance song. The whole way home, I watched out the van window taking in the beauty of the mountains with that song playing repeatedly in my mind.

Before we returned home from New York, we realized we would be close to one of our favorite churches in Silver Spring, MD. Immanuel's was our annual fall retreat gathering place. We would rent a missionary building nearby each October and spend the weekend refueling our spirits at the church's conference.

It was early evening when we decided to swing by and see what was happening there. When we entered the lobby, the Pastor's wife greeted us and there were hugs all around. Our timing was perfect because they were just about to start their evening service.

Since we were 'frequent attendees' at women's events, she invited us to take part in the Parade of the Nations, they often did before services began. She explained that all we needed to do was choose a flag from the ones rolled up along the wall and join a line of flag bearers that were waiting to take the flags to the front of the church during the processional. I was really excited! What an honor!

So, we hurried to where the flags were placed, grabbed one, and rushed to get in line because the music was beginning. As we took our places, we realized that we had to unroll our flags. Quickly, we spun them to their full size.

As I saw my flag, my mouth fell open, and tears welled within my eyes. I almost missed the cue to start walking.

I carried the flag of the American Indians, a part of whom I was and whom He was calling me to become- a MIGHTY WARRIOR!

He is THE MASTER OF TIMING AND DELIVERY! He only requires that we BE STILL AND KNOW THAT HE IS GOD! There are NO coincidences and NO mistakes.

THE TIMING OF EVERY MOMENT IS IN HIS HANDS!

# THE MASTER PRUNER

John 15:2 discusses the process of 'pruning' that each Christian must face in the hands of the Master Pruner.

*'He cuts off every branch in me that bears no fruit, while every branch that does bear fruit, He prunes so that it will be even more fruitful.*

One of my least favorite activities as a teacher, were formal observations. I disliked them, even more than parent conferences! Year after year, we were subjected to this process no matter how many years of teaching experience we had.

I never slept the night before and spent countless hours planning and refining every aspect of the lesson.

I was blessed to work under several administrators who made this experience less painful by taking part in my 'engagement' activities that often began lessons using humor or humorous stories.

One that still makes me laugh, was a kindergarten lesson on shapes. I had gathered certain objects in a box, to share with the children who sat facing me. My administrators sat behind my back, where the box was sitting on a student desk. As we discussed each object, the children began to squeal in glee, as they watched our principal quietly find and add more objects to the box! There's nothing compared to the joy of children's delight!

After each lesson was taught, a post-observation conference was held. Each administrator took turns sharing the "marks of a well-developed lesson" they observed, and the responses they heard from the students. We followed a checklist, to highlight necessary elements and how they were implemented. Then, came the hardest part for me; the suggestions they felt would have improved its presentation or success.

It wasn't the hardest part because I felt there was no need for improvement on my end. It was painful because I had invested so much into the entire process from the beginning. My heart and soul were poured into each piece; I based certain elements on the specific needs of my students. It almost became a part of me, as an instructor. To have someone else 'cut away,' at my finished work, was exceedingly difficult. If I could agree that their suggestions were indeed a better path to student success, that made those suggestions easier to accept. However, that didn't seem to happen as often as I would have liked.

When we submit ourselves to the Master's pruning, those same feelings come into play. He would not be a loving Father, if He were not allowed to 'cut away' those things that are not healthy or best for us.

At those moments, we don't always see things through His eyes. Many times, we dig in our heels and refuse to make the changes He is requiring.

As time goes on, some people will begin to see His perspective but their anger, fear, or need to be right continues to keep them from allowing those necessary cuttings to take place. Sometimes, we mistakenly allow those necessary prunings, to define who we are, instead of allowing the Pruner to continue to shape and mold, who we are to become.

As I have shared in other stories within this book, I was a proud member of a Women's Ministry group for 12 years. I had attended several retreats and conferences before this time and met many of the ladies who were members of this ministry at those events. I was mesmerized by their level of faith and experiences with the Lord.

They warmly welcomed me into their ministry and I easily found a place to grow in my faith and love of God. During that time, He helped me in many ways to heal, to believe, to love, and to begin to trust. The leaders watched me grow and gave me increased opportunities to serve within the ministry. Before long, I was writing, composing, teaching, preaching, and performing.

Life was full and good. Tom quietly watched with some concern, yet he gave me room, to grow increasingly in love with the Lord.

Then, in May of 2008, my Mom went home to be with the Lord. While she had been sick all her life with us, and we knew how frail she was, I still wasn't prepared for the full impact of her loss. God had given her the gift of total healing and eternal peace, as she entered the gates of heaven. While I knew that, the way others handled my loss, shook the foundation of who I had become. It was the beginning of a pruning that God had divinely timed.

After her funeral, I was stunned at what I was feeling and thoughts that seemed to never give me rest. The anger that was unleashed within me toward my father was frightening. I knew better than to let it get a stronghold within me. My close friend and counselor Deb and I began to work on it even as I sat in the car on the morning of my Mom's passing. While my closest ministry partners knew what I was walking through, no one stopped at the hospice, sat with me, and let me know that I wasn't alone. I had given so much of myself to this group and didn't understand why there were so few available for me. One sister told me that she felt the Holy Spirit moving her to visit me the night before my Mom went home, but decided to let the opportunity pass. In some ways, it was like experiencing the abandonments of growing up all over again. My efforts at finding answers, were falling painfully short.

The one place, I did find comfort, was at our church listening to our Pastor who was masterfully trained at sharing the Word of God. God was at work; He knew I needed to believe what was shared was truth, His truth.

One Sunday evening, we were listening to our Pastor share the story of the healings of Jesus. He specifically cited the time that people carried a man on a mat to the home where Jesus was healing others. When they arrived, they found no way to get inside. Not to be deterred, they began to take apart the straw roof on the house and lowered the man into the home for his healing.

What I didn't know was that when Jesus speaks to the man after he is healed, He directs him to not go back the way he came. It was as if a wooden beam hit me across the chest. It took my breath away. I knew exactly what God was saying to me in that moment. "Do not go back the way you came."

I knew what He meant. After twelve years of ministry with these ladies whom I had served and loved, He was telling me to come away. It was His direction that I be pruned off that vine. It was devastating. I had such an investment in that ministry, and as I said earlier, I loved these ladies and this ministry. It had defined who I had become. And that was exactly where the problem lay.

You see, instead of becoming what He wanted me to become, I had allowed myself to be shaped by what the others wanted me to be. That wasn't their fault. I had placed all my belief in them instead of Him. I lived for their approval, and not His. While my intention was to be who He wanted me to be, I had allowed my relationship with Him, to be an outgrowth of my relationship with the people in the ministry.

If you don't already know it, God is a jealous God- He deserves and expects to hold top bill in your life. (Deuteronomy 4:23-24) This was my notice - I want top bill in your life, Michele. It was time for a one-to-one covenant, not one lived through others.

I allowed Him to prune that part of my life away. It wasn't easy, but I knew it was the right thing to do and I persevered just as those men did to put that man through the roof of the house.

I have watched God birth in me a greater measure of gifts that were in their infant stages years ago. He has truly brought forth more fruit from those branches of my life. Pruning is often painful but necessary, especially if your sincere desire is to be all that He has created you to become.

*"For I know the plans I have for you, declares the Lord, plans to prosper you and not to harm you, plans to give you a hope and a future." - Jeremiah 29:11*

# HE MAKES HIMSELF KNOWN

When the Lord gave me the teaching for the Seven Keys of Healing, He also gave me the color for each key on the key ring. After He shared the colors, He added words as well.

I have this habit of trying to figure Him out before He shares reasons with me. I had some rather clever ideas, as to why He chose white for the first key color. None of them, compared to what I heard.

*"Put the words,* **Desperate Desire** *on the first key."*

I was left wondering at those two words. Then, the reason came.

The first step to true healing begins with a desperate desire to change from your present state. It is a desire to be healthier or whole. It requires a conscious decision to move in a different direction. You often hear people say that they hit rock bottom before their lives turned around. This is very much the same.

It was coming together, but why white?

The next thing He showed me, was a picture of a morning drive to the school I taught at. That morning, the interstate I traveled on from Pennsylvania to Riderwood, my school, had become completely covered in ice in a matter of twenty minutes. I was heading onto the ramp for the interstate, unaware of what had happened. Cars were already flipped on their sides in the median and grassy spots. I gripped the steering wheel and prayed. That was at 7:05 a.m.

At 11:30 a.m., I arrived in the school office into the arms of my principal, who held me tight as I cried like a baby. Then, as she took my hands, I was shocked to see that my knuckles and joints were white and hurting. I had held that steering wheel so tight for the whole trip and my hands were a memory of what had happened.

After this vision, the Lord told me:

*When we land at the end of a path and are desperate to find relief, it is as if we have been on a 'white-knuckle journey' holding on with all that we have- until there's nothing left but Him.*

As I reflect on the events of my life, I can point to the moments when I was indeed in a "white-knuckle" situation. With heartfelt gratitude, I can also share the witness of my faithful Father in each of those moments. I have shared quite a few of them, within these ponderings. I hope you will allow me the pleasure of sharing one more!

At the end of the year that I made my half-day journey to school on the ice, God supplied a new position in a school closer to our home. It was also in a specific zone that closes more often, because of dangerous weather! Hallelujah!

While at that school, I was working with my counselor Deb on trust, an issue that I had struggled with all my life. We were heading into territory I wasn't sure I could handle. Laying open lies for what they truly are, can be challenging for the strongest of souls.

One morning, I worked my way around the room sitting with each student to revise their work. I was scheduled to meet Deb after school. I felt the desperation rising within me.

In my nervousness, I was fingering a bracelet that I was wearing. I received it from my Christmas secret sister at church that year. It was a lovely design in two colors of gold.

As I was fingering the bracelet, I heard myself saying over and over, "Lord I really need to know You are with me". My fingers traced over the design several times, before I looked down and gasped, as I saw that it wasn't a design at all.

There were three letters- G-O-D! Instantly, my heart was full, and a smile rolled across my face. His word says, *"you will seek Me and find Me when you seek Me with all of your heart."* (Jeremiah 29:13)

Remember, you are not alone within a 'white-knuckle' moment, unless you choose to go it alone. We have a plaque hanging in our home that says, "Help is just a prayer away." Spend some time with your Savior - He's also the owner of the "Comfort Inn!"

*The view from my wrist.*

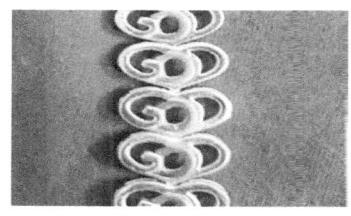

*My Father's view*

# "NEVER TO ME, I DECLARED!"

There aren't many times we are allowed to challenge the Lord. One that you should be familiar with, involves tithes and offerings. Many folks choose to ignore this scripture because they cannot reason the giving of a tenth of what they have or earn to the Lord. Their reasons fall short of His intention. They will tell you that He has no need of it. He, however, sees it as an act of obedience. He uses it as a pathway to blessing His children.

My husband Tom and I have witnessed the Lord's blessings and those of so many others over the years, because of faithfulness in tithing. It's quite easy to profess the benefits of something, when life is good and anxieties don't include finances. Our blessings have most often come when our pockets were woefully empty!

There was a long banner that was always displayed in my classroom, no matter how many times I had to move to a new place in the schoolhouse. It was from the Bible, but I had easily clipped the biblical reference off, before putting it at the top of the wall. It read, "Stand up for what is right, even if you're the only one standing." Many children referred to that banner as they dealt with the day-to-day challenges of growing up and finding their place, within their age-mates.

As an adult, Tom has had to stand firm in many work-places and has paid a large price for his integrity and re-fusal to lower his standards. Years ago, he lamented every night about his inability to continue to follow the lead of others, he knew were out of line. We prayed and talked about the consequences of taking that stand. Not long af-ter, he was without a job.

While we were shaken, we held onto the Lord, who had our backs. Some hours were easy, others were ter-rifying. We were approaching spring and then summer; the hardest financial time for teachers. I found myself becoming angrier and put-off by those whose lives con-tinued around us, without any concern about what had happened to Tom and me.

Then, one Sunday morning, we sat and listened to our dear Pastor introduce a visiting Pastor, who had held revival services all around the world. He was the guest speaker, and our church prepared to ask each of us to commit to an annual mission offering. "Not the right timing for this member," I thought to myself. "You have got to be kidding!"

The Pastor continued about people in the past who had reluctantly written an amount on their pledge and were astounded by the Lord's faithfulness to fulfilling that pledge. "Right," I murmured. "That might happen to other people, but that would never happen to me!"

At the end of the sermon, the Pastor again asked ev-eryone to pray. Tom and I prayed together. We looked at each other with uncertainty and disbelief. How could we possibly commit to an amount, when we didn't know how we were going to make ends meet each week?

Surprisingly, we both heard the same amount. It only made the situation more unreasonable! "One thousand dollars? Really God - are you kidding?" I thought. "Whatever." I resigned myself with a shrug of my shoulder. It was only a number on a piece of paper.

Little did we know, God had challenged us to believe what He had spoken to us.

On Friday of that week, we received a check in the mail from our mortgage company. It was for a little more than a thousand dollars. Our escrow account had an excess and they returned it to us. I laughed and cried at the same time as I carried it into the house for Tom to see.

Now, however, there was a new challenge. God had confirmed to both of us that He had given us an amount. It was now our turn to give that money to the missions' fund in fulfillment of our promise. It WAS NOT easy. That money would have given us a safety cushion. We both knew what had to be done and it was easier for Tom than for me.

I decided to make it impossible for me to back out and hold on to the money. I wrote to our Pastor and shared the story assuring him that the check for our pledge, would be in the offering that Sunday.

The following week, God put the icing on the cake so to speak. We received another letter from the mortgage company explaining that our monthly mortgage payment would be reduced for the following year by one-twelfth of the excess we had received. Over the next year, we would receive an added savings of a monthly payment because of the adjustment.

God not only gave us our commitment once to give to missions, He also gave us that amount because of our obedience to Him.

NEVER say NEVER to the Lord. It's a no-no. Especially when He is involved in the equation. In Malachi 3, verse 10, God makes it very clear what He will do when we are obedient to what He asks of us. We can challenge that in different ways. He is always faithful to His Word. We are proof of it!

# HE NEVER FORGETS

As we age, (gracefully), our memory begins to lose its accuracy and simple things like a name or number become harder to retrieve from that magnificent filing cabinet, we've relied on for years.

Even though we saw this decline in our parents, I was completely unprepared for what happened to Tom as he went through an experience that folks call, 'chemo brain.'

It began, right after his eye surgeries and I initially thought it was because of being under anesthesia for the six plus hours, he was on the operating table. As fellow pranksters, there was a moment, that I thought he was pulling my leg.

Then, at a doctor's visit, I asked about my concern. That's when the new issue was explained. Fortunately, it usually goes away after chemotherapy ends. You can imagine how this affected us, as he struggled to remember the events from even just one hour earlier.

\*

Our Creator NEVER forgets even the simplest prayer

placed at His feet. He keeps track of the tears we cry and celebrates with us over every accomplishment. We are promised His undivided attention and He will never leave or forsake us. (Deuteronomy 31:6-8)

He never tires from our conversation, even when we repeatedly bring the same burdens before Him. As I have witnessed and ministered to others, I hear them complain that either God doesn't listen or remember their petitions. Neither is true.

We must remember His position in our lives. As Creator, He understands every intricate piece of our being. He must occupy a position of significance. Just as parents, and even teachers, must make unpopular decisions for those in their care, God also has to say 'no' at times in our lives.

I personally believe that it's not always easy for Him to do. However, unlike us, He knows the outcome beforehand, so there is no margin of error for Him. It took me time to be able to move past noes believing and trusting that He had a better outcome. It is in many ways, a time-tested process. It gets easier as time goes on.

Each of the events that I am going to share with you, serve as a testimony that HE DOES INDEED listen and remember prayers given to Him. Their realization took time and were completely without expectation, at the time of their fulfillment.

One more thought; if or when God places something on your heart to carry out, please follow through. As you will see from these ponderings, the actions of others were key to their fulfillment. I am indeed doubly blessed that they were obedient!

\*

In the mid 2000's, I was really beginning to be fatigued with everything that was needed to work through difficulties and receive healing. There was no way I was giving up; I was only tired.

I clearly remember one afternoon, asking God with my eyes raised upward, why He couldn't just open the 'lid of my head,' take out the misfiring circuit board, and replace it with a brand new one! Sounds crazy, doesn't it? I laughed as I pictured it and went on with my day.

Years later, we were hosting a worship band at our evening service that was led by a young adult who had come from our church. I had heard his band before at an outdoor 'Jesus in the Park' concert, and encouraged Tom to join me for the event. He agreed to listen to the band and asked if we could leave after worship so he could get his necessary rest for the week of work ahead.

While the band was popular, I was genuinely surprised to see that the church's sanctuary was packed, when we arrived. We took seats near the back, so as not to disturb others when leaving. The lights were dimmed to provide an atmosphere of worship and the songs played ushered those hungry souls into the presence of the King!

Sometime during this time, I leaned over to Tom and whispered that I didn't remember the band having a young lady as a lead singer, when I had first heard them. While I hated to leave, we slowly walked to the back doors as the music ended and the band members headed to their seats. Just outside the sanctuary doors, the band leader and the girl who had led songs, called to catch our attention. I was surprised and couldn't believe that the leader remembered me. He didn't.

The young lady quite nervously said to me, "I know you don't know me, but God asked me to tell you something. I don't have any idea what this means, but I'm sure that it will mean something to you. He said to tell you that He is exchanging your circuit board with a brand new one." Not only had He heard, He made sure that I heard His answer. HE DOES LISTEN!

\*

I was honored to be the guest of a dear friend at a women's conference held at her church called, 'Beloved.' Its focus, was showering women with the love that Christ has for His church, His bride.

Women spend countless amounts of time preparing for their own weddings and key aspects of this event highlighted, how we, as His church, prepare for His return. Each attendee even received a silver wedding band from Israel that was engraved with the word, 'Beloved.'

On the last day, as we sang songs of adoration, a man dressed as Jesus walked onto the platform. Now that may not sound very climatic, but this man is often asked to portray Jesus by area churches because of His appearance.

At first, there was a gasp followed by silence. Then, quiet weeping could be heard. We were, at that moment, being silently asked what we would do, when He stood before us. Then, one of the leaders, invited us to approach Him, one by one.

The Holy Spirit took charge and the presence of God was clear. As we finished, we were invited to a gathering room, where we received our rings. Then, we passed through two doors, to a hall, that had been turned into a wedding reception hall.

It was breathtaking! Everything was decorated in white and gold. It was extravagant in every way! The men of the church served us and I was truly blessed to be invited to sit with my friend and other women leaders of the church. There were two other ladies at the table who lead a separate ministry, that I had met earlier. We had shared testimonies several times before. I felt a bit special, to be sitting with a group of people that I admired and respected in their faith walks.

After the dinner dishes were removed, 'Jesus' reappeared and the speakers shared that he was going to cut the wedding cake. It was spectacular! Earlier, we had all walked over and gushed over its beauty.

There was a quiet buzz in the room as at least two hundred eyes watched him cut that first piece and place it on the plate. After placing a fork next to it, he turned and began walking.

Then, the whispering began about who would be getting that first piece of cake! There were giggles and giddiness as he walked across the floor.

I didn't even look up. I'm not sure why, except that I was sure it wouldn't be me. When he turned at our table, it appeared he was heading for one of the better-known ladies sitting there. But then, he stopped right behind my chair. Gently, he laid the plate in front of me and smiled in a way that warmed my heart.

While that was absolutely astounding, in and of itself, the best was what came next. All the ladies at my table and the tables surrounding ours, began chatting about their not getting the first piece and that I must be someone incredibly special. They even joked about getting me a license plate with a similar sentiment.

I blushed and laughed, but then as if an old record were put on to play, I reasoned that the portrayer already knew me from working together in a *Heaven's Gates and Hell's Flames* production together. That was why he picked me.

I left my seat and went over to thank him for the first piece of cake. During that quick conversation, he denied I received the cake because he knew me. The Holy Spirit had directly instructed him to deliver it to me.

That's when I realized that my King was giving me a gift, I had waited for all my life- to feel important, special, singled out, not left out. He had remembered all those times in my life that I had tried so hard to 'make the grade,' be the focus of attention, and feel the affection of someone that others would envy.

I recognized it was an exchange between He and I, divinely orchestrated and timed to touch my heart. I knew the others were only having an enjoyable time, knowing full well they were priceless to the King, just as He had shown me. He was implicitly telling me, 'You are mine!" HE NEVER FORGOT!

That leaves us with the vital key at the end of the 'Faith in God' pondering. Will you choose to believe? I hope you will- He is faithful!

# BENEATH IT ALL

Genesis 1:27 tells us that God created us in His own image. When we think of an image of something, our minds create a picture. However, when God created us, His image was not to make us physically look like Him. God plants within us aspects of Himself to create an inward connection between the Creator and the created.

The stirring believers feel that there is something deeper than just "living life," or that there is a "purpose for their being," are the hints of those pieces of God within us. How these stirrings are nurtured, determine the depth of the relationship we develop with our Creator.

I would like to ask you to humor me for just a moment. Think about those interesting machines that spit out tennis balls to folks practicing on the courts. You can always tell how skilled players are by watching their ability to handle those yellow spheres lobbed at them without ceasing. Can you picture the highest-level player? Easily, they handle each pitch.

Medium-level players do well also, but they seem to show their wear quicker. Lower-level players miss two balls for every one they successfully meet. They will often begin to joke about the game in an effort to distract anyone watching. The last group has no experience with the skills required for the game or how to pace oneself to endure the challenge. Can you imagine how the game begins and how they react to each ball that comes speeding in their direction?

Having shared this analogy, I would now like you to substitute the tennis balls hurled toward the players, for the daily experiences of life.

We all know people in our lives who appear to have it all together. They take life in stride, and for all on-lookers, seem to have few hurdles to clear.

The middle group does well, too. They have good lives, work hard, are well-liked, and may not always get it right all the time, but their efforts secure the approval of others.

Our lower-level players sometimes try hard and sometimes are too worn to give anymore. Frequently they start again with the best of intentions trying to learn from what has happened before.

Our final group of friends, come to the court with all that appears to be needed to play. However, no one has shown them the necessary skills to play the game. The balls begin and they are left to figure out what to do so that they are not a moving target for this relentless machine.

While it may be funny to watch, it is definitely not fun to live this way. That is how people feel who struggle with mental health issues. Some come into the world with these issues, others are beaten down for years by those 'yellow balls of life' and can no longer get up one more time.

I cannot explain why these people suffer so much. I do know God desires to have an intimate relationship with every one of them. While I have no scientific data to prove my next proposition, I would imagine it to be true.

Most people find that they "need" God when their lives are out-of-control. So, it becomes hard to imagine those "got-it-all-together-folks" would have need of an intimate relationship with Him.

Our middle and lower-level friends become desperate to fix or change the circumstances around them when things get tougher. They will often grow angry or bitter when answers are not easy or swift. The relationship with God that they depend on is untested, lacking in fervor, with little to no foundation. All these components are straightforwardly corrected, a relationship with Jesus nurtured with time and love.

Our last group of friends have had to deal with hurdles often. So, they might try their absolute best to meet them head on. Sometimes they are successful, sometimes they fail.

Amid this process, they may also realize they do not have all they need to be successful. This is a key realization. Some of these souls are the ones who have learned how to search for the answer, go deeper, or not surrender to the onslaught of difficulties. They dig down beneath all the surface distractions and seek Him who is at the heart of their peace and solitude. His grace and mercy covers them in comfort and gives them the strength to be still and know.

✳

Eric was indeed a man after God's own heart. You could see the joy of the Lord in his eyes. His smile and kindness were larger than life. He was special in my eyes from the moment I met him. His Mom was kind enough to let me think of him as my own son.

Eric loved to capture God's world through the lens of his camera. The pictures he took were breathtaking and captured the uniqueness of creation.

His love of music and the guitar held a large piece of his heart as well. He used that gift to sing praises to His Father and create songs of worship and adoration. His guitar was like another arm- he always sought time with it.

Before graduation from college, Eric began to experience some health issues that drew concern from his parents. He seemed different, troubled, far away, and argumentative. While many avenues were explored to determine the cause for the changes, a definitive answer was never determined.

Life became increasingly more difficult for Eric to handle. He struggled to maintain daily routines and experiences, although he gave it his all. There were those who stood by his side and others who when they could not comprehend the issues, walked away.

Eric was never able to walk away from his life or what he endured inside his mind. However, the one precious piece of Eric's mind that he had nurtured, poured his love over, and spent hours cultivating, was his intimate love relationship with His Father. He could count on peace there. Beneath all the pain and torture, he endured in his mind, was that private refuge that belonged to him and His Creator.

Eric left us many gifts. His music and photography still bless those who listen to his worship songs and ponder over what he captured with his camera. One of Eric's finest gifts, is the essential priority to create a secret refuge to spend time with Our Creator daily. His desire to work to find Him even in his most desperate hours, teaches us that it does not matter how far we must dig or how much time we have to offer, that relationship is paramount to living this life in victory. Not as the world sees victory, but as God sees it in His image.

# YOUR TRUE DWELLING PLACE

*Don't give up tomorrow,*
*Because of what you dwell on today.*

*Memories are just that,*
*A snapshot of the past.*
*Some pleasant,*
*Some very painful - but*

*They can't change today.*
*And most of us allow them,*
*To steal our tomorrows,*
*By dwelling on*
*What might have been.*

*Your power and control over them,*
*Were also just a snapshot in the past.*

*God is in charge - here and now,*
*Let Him shape the tomorrows of your life.*
*He's much better at it than you are!*

✳

### Psalm 84:1, 4, 12

*How lovely is your dwelling place, O Lord Almighty!*

*Blessed are those who dwell in your house: they are ever praising You.*

*O, Lord, Almighty, blessed is the man who trusts in You.*

# CLOSING THOUGHTS

Many times, along this path, I have been told that God is a gentleman. I share this thought with you, because it is important to understand that healing begins in the hands of the hurting. When I crashed early in my life, I was told it had happened because all the coping mechanisms I had put in place, did not work anymore. I knew, down deep inside, there was a healthier, happier way to live.

I also, truly believe, people are ready for this journey when it hurts bad enough and they believe there is a better path - the Lord. The length of time they are on their journey will depend on how much they are willing to honestly examine and work on their issues.

Within each episode of my healing victories, God waited for me to be ready and willing to take the next step. There were too many moments where I dug in my heels, or was just too afraid to go forward and see what was there, causing me so much pain. Gently, He worked with me to tackle each wound, scar, and lie. Some of them, were decades old. Some, remain to be healed. It took time. The wounds and mistruths that I carried with me, occurred over years of my life. Their resolution took years as well, but it was the best time that I have ever invested in myself!

One of the precious gifts that Deb taught me, was to ask God where He was amid the heartaches that I experienced. This is a vital key. Be sure to ask Him the same question when you are working on healing. His response about His presence always brought me to tears and gave me the peace of knowing I was not there alone. I can assure you He has been with you in your valleys, too.

I remember often praying as a young girl, for God to rescue me, as I stood in our basement. Just as in the movie, *Pretty Woman*, where Richard Gere comes as a knight to rescue Julia Roberts, God sent me Tom, my own precious knight. He bravely carried me off with his covenant promise of affection and attention. His deep sense of commitment and compassion were the perfect examples of what I would later learn, were attributes of my heavenly Father.

I would also like to talk to you for a few minutes about forgiveness. This can be a difficult subject for people to consider. They, as was I, are sure that no one can understand the pain they have experienced, if you are asking them to forgive those who they hold responsible.

It was a steep mountain for me to climb. I had adamantly shared with my Mom that I would not be visiting my father when she had gone home. God, however, had a different plan.

It was my desire to act the way God would have expected, that brought me to calling my father several times a month. As a result of long calls and discussions about faith, I was able to lead him in prayer to the promise that he, would indeed, see my mother again in heaven. During a call sometime later, he asked me to forgive him for the way he had treated me growing up.

I told him that I already had. He said that he was not surprised because he knew that was the way I was. Then, I shared I had not forgiven him on my own or because of his request. I had done it in obedience to my Father in heaven, because that was what He expected of me.

I listened to a Pastor at our church who once shared that unforgiveness is like drinking a poison and expecting someone else to die. Think about that. We hold onto pain and hurts for prolonged periods of time. They become toxic to and within us.

How long do the people who have hurt us suffer because of what they have done to us? I will give you a hint - most of the time, not very long! Sometimes, they are oblivious to the suffering we endure. The true reason for forgiving them is even simpler than this.

Earlier in this book, I mentioned a part of the Lord's Prayer. Listen to another vital piece:

*"And forgive us our debts as we forgive our debtors."*

In other words, we cannot be forgiven, unless we release others. Another place in scripture, tells us to pray for our enemies. Please understand - I am not saying this is an easy task! However, when your purpose is to be obedient to the Lord and humble yourself before Him, the ability to succeed becomes easier.

There were times when I had to repeatedly tell the Lord that I had forgiven someone, because in my heart. I wanted them to hurt like they hurt me. It became a declaration of forgiveness until my heart would finally let go. That tipping point was my longing to please God and not my flesh. I also experienced forgiving someone for their actions against me, only to have them turn around and hurt me many more times. How are we expected to respond to this? Jesus says in Matthew 18:21-22, we should forgive seventy times seven. Easy? Absolutely not! Yet, another act of obedience to Him who holds my everything - including His protection over me from future pain.

This does not include anything that can be described as abuse in any form. No one is expected to endure anything in that regard, without seeking professional help. In addition, God does not intend for His children to continually put themselves in circumstances they know will cause pain. He expects us to use wisdom.

There were also times when the enemy would rear his ugly head and remind me of a hurt from the past. Having already settled that hurt with the Lord, it allowed me to send the enemy off to discuss it with Him! I simply said, "That's not an issue anymore. I have already taken care of it with the Lord. If you have a problem with that, take it up with the Him!"

Lauren Daigle's song, *You Say*, captures so perfectly to whom I belong and in whom I find my value and importance. God has lovingly led me through countless times of healing and trust. It has become my greatest desire, to live in a way that makes Him proud of His daughter. His covenant with me, is far too important to allow bitterness to choke our relationship. Instead of using my time with Him to revisit why I should be allowed to hold others in a prison of unforgiveness and anger, I understand that time is far too valuable to waste. He has taught me how to gain 'the peace that surpasses understanding' through the time I devote to Him. His word says in Romans 12:19 KJV, "*Vengeance is mine! I will repay.*" I commit to Him, the things that are His to handle. As a result, I keep my hands clean and continue to enjoy my covenant with my Savior!

Finally, I had to chuckle, as I pondered this section of the book. I found my thoughts returning to *Pretty Woman*. Julia Roberts had been shunned and ridiculed, as she tried to shop for clothes for an important occasion with Richard Gere. Later in the film, she returns to the same shop with a handful of credit cards and shopping bags. She asks those same salespeople if they work on commission. They do, of course. Then, with a smile larger than life, she flashes her purchases and announces that they have made, *a big mistake - a huge mistake* not waiting on her the day before.

I cannot imagine there is anyone who cannot glory in that moment for Julia Roberts! We are so much more than what is outwardly evident! God knows every one of His distinct creations perfectly.

I smiled as I thought about the Lord and His endless love and work throughout my life. I stopped, for just a moment, and reflected on the people, who, in the past, sold me short. Some, because they never looked further than the surface or their own desires. There was no regard for the pain I endured as a result of their actions. God called them shallow. Others' actions highlighted the struggle with their own painful pasts and shortcomings. These resulted in their repeated attempts to pull me down and keep me there. This is a perfect example of the expression, "Hurting people hurt people." While understandable, not acceptable.

Then, I pictured the Lord, as He sits on His throne. He never doubted I would be what He had destined me to become. He walked hand-in-hand with me, securing each step of my healing. He taught me to trust again with confidence because He knows what is best for me. We have shared so many precious moments together that are secure within my heart. Despite all I went through, strived to be, and worked to overcome; I was always His!

I believe He may have even laughed at some of the people in my past and commented on their actions saying, "Big mistake! Huge mistake! She is mine!"

# THE IMPORTANCE OF MUSIC

The healing exchanges you have with Jesus will be personally catered to you. The tools He uses to help you along the way, will be just as unique. Pay attention to what you pray and how He answers the desires of your heart. He knows each intricate part of your being and will design each healing path, based on what He knows you specifically need.

For me, music was key! The kind of music He used was unique to each part of my healing journeys. There were songs that took me back to my childhood and solidified the ageless truths about Him that were integral to that moment. There were songs that allowed me to declare the pain and heartbreaks of the past and how deep that pain went within me. Others, named those broken pieces and declared that He indeed, oversaw their restoration.

My favorite songs were the ones that worshipped and adored Him for who He was in my life. Times of pure reverence, worship, and a humble spirit when I was poured out before Him. In those pieces of time, the rest of the world disappeared, and I had His total attention and affection. It was an exchange of pure love between the King and His daughter. Moments that belonged to only me. Forever mine! The only time in my life, I looked forward to being alone - with Him!

Below is a list of some of my favorite healing songs. They may help to get you started if you need some ideas. Remember, it should not be that hard. Quiet your spirit and listen.

Songs to enjoy on your healing journey:

1. You Raise Me Up – Josh Groban
2. He Knows - Jeremy Camp
3. You Say - Lauren Daigle
4. Shoulders - For King and Country
5. In the Garden
6. Great Is Thy Faithfulness
7. How Great Thou Art
8. Even If – Mercy Me
9. Dear Younger Me - Mercy Me
10. Amazing Grace - My Chains are Gone
11. Oceans - Where Feet May Fail- Hillsong United
12. Blessed Assurance
13. I Will Rise - Chris Tomlin
14. Look Up Child - Lauren Daigle
15. Waymaker - Leeland
16. Trust in You - Lauren Daigle
17. Agnus Dei - Michael W. Smith
18. Dance with Me – Paul Wilbur
19. In Your Presence - Paul Wilbur
20. Beautiful - Mercy Me
21. Pretty Woman - Roy Orbison (It always makes me smile when I hear it!)

22. Lady - Kenny Rogers (Tom's song to me at our wedding & 40<sup>th</sup> anniversary celebration)
23. You Light Up My Life - Debby Boone (My song to Tom)
24. Battles - The Afters
25. Revelation Song - Phillips, Craig, and Dean
26. God Only Knows - for King and Country
27. Worthy of It All- Onething Live & Lauren Alexandria Dueck
28. Tis So Sweet to Trust in Jesus - Casting Crowns
29. The Potter's Hand – Dalene Joyce Zschech
30. Terry Macalman - his songs are amazing!
31. Rise Up Mighty Warrior - Broken Walls - Jonathan Maracle
32. Broken Hallelujah - The Afters
33. Well Done - The Afters

# HEALING JOURNEY ESSENTIALS

As with any journey, having the right supplies prepares the traveler for whatever may occur. I find the following "must have" items have blessed me countless times and I am quite certain they will serve you well!

1. A **Bible** that is easy to read and understand. (You will find the more time you spend in the Word, the easier it will become!)

2. A **journal**. See the Faith in God pondering.

3. A **quiet place** where you can rely on undisturbed time.

4. Plenty of **music**. In whatever form you can enjoy it as you seek God. I had favorites that were played repeatedly because they spoke directly to my hurting soul. This includes instruments you play!

5. A **pad for drawing**. More than once, God gave me pictures to help me understand what He was teaching me.

6. A **dictionary**. Use the one on your phone. God has given me words when I have prayed about a topic or issue. There are times that I am aware of a word, but am led to check the definition for His purpose.

7. Lots of **tissues**. Invest in them!
8. A **trusted friend** in whom you know you can confide. Pray about this person and wait until God places someone in your path or on your heart. Watch and listen to those around you - let the Holy Spirit guide your choice. You will know!

Your confidant will help you along the way as you spend time with the Lord and share issues to gain healing. If you need professional help, seek the guidance of your Pastor or your trusted friend. There is no shame in needing help, only healing!

Made in the USA
Las Vegas, NV
02 October 2021

31563930R00C83